THE HEART OF SERVANTHOOD

THE HEART

Of

SERVANTHOOD

The Purpose Of Mankind
Is Found In Servanthood

ALISON MARCELLUS

XULON ELITE

Xulon Press
2301 Lucien Way #415
Maitland, FL 32751
407.339.4217
www.xulonpress.com

Paperback ISBN-13: 978-1-6628-6922-8
Ebook ISBN-13: 978-1-6628-6924-2

Contents

Commitment is "an agreement or pledge to do something in the future," "an engagement to assume a financial obligation at a future date," "something pledged," and "an act of committing to a charge or trust: such as an act of referring a matter to a legislative committee." Commitment is the foundation of any relationship in a healthy life. It involves dedicating yourself to something, a person or a cause. Commitment obligates you to do something. The best way to describe commitment and make it visible to your imagination is with the example of marriage. In a marriage, there is a vow between both parties that states this contract is for a lifetime. The longevity of the agreement is part of the vow, so you have the idea "to have and to hold from this day forward, for better, for worse, for richer, for poorer, for sickness, and in health, to love and to cherish, till death do us part." The phrase "*Till death do us part* can't get more definite on the longevity of the vow. These words show us that challenges will arise. You will, no doubt, be blindsided by a trial at one time or another, and surprising circumstances will occur. Commitment withstands all weaknesses, insecurities, and disadvantages.

Commitment is not a race. It is a marathon. When things are going well you will never be confronted with commitment. But when things become ugly or uncomfortable, that's when commitment becomes crucial. Only in adverse situations is commitment validated, expressed, or reaffirmed. When you're committed in difficult situations, there's a revelation of yourself. Yes, that's right—how you act when things get tough brings out your real character. But how can commitment become a lifestyle in your life? The answer is in the renewing of the mind, mentioned in Romans 12:2. "*And be not conformed to this world; but be transformed by the*

Foreword

The art of serving others has been lost over time, and more recent generations can certainly attest to this. Although still relevant, service is hardly practiced in modern times, but it is often tainted with wrong motives and bad attitudes. The concept of service has been degenerating to the point that servers are seen as an inferior class, which comes as a terrible consequence of pride. Service is no longer seen as one of the essential principles of the kingdom of God. In addition, some people serve wholeheartedly, but for one reason or another, they have not been able to persevere in their service; consequently, they could not reap the entire harvest of what they have sown. In my book, *The Towel of Service,* I state that every believer is called to serve God and His people. The word *servant* comes from the Greek *"Doulos,"* which is attributed to someone with a permanent attitude of service to others. A faithful servant is one who does his work continually, without faltering and does it well. Jesus was a *"Doulos"* He did not think of Himself; instead, His mind and heart remained focused on serving His neighbor. He gave Himself entirely to others. If every believer understood the true meaning of what it represents to be part of the body of Christ, they would give more importance to the gift God has given us. As parts of the same body, we are called to be united, be an example, and a light upon the earth, as Jesus was. For *"the Son of Man did not come to be served, but to serve"* (Matt. 20:28). I recognize that the principle of service is deeply linked to the principle of authority. That is why I am pleased to write a foreword for a leader such as Alison Marcellus, a dear son of our church in Miami. He is dedicated to serving others as Jesus did and imparting the revelation that God's people need. Hence, anyone who seeks positions of authority in any field of life must first learn to put on the towel of service and give themselves to help others. Jesus teaches us that *"whoever wishes to be first among you shall be your servant"* (Matt. 20:27). In this verse, Jesus tells us that if anyone wishes to become a leader, overseer, or even head of state, they must first serve those they want to rule. True greatness does not lie in ruling over the people but in being the *"Doulos"* or servant. Alison's book *The Heart of Servanthood*, gives us the keys we need to know what it means to have the heart of a servant. After reading this book, I sincerely believe that your mind will change and be spiritually restored and transformed! Let us carry out the work that Jesus commanded us to do on earth while loving and serving God and our neighbor as we would ourselves. Blessings,

—*Apostle Guillermo Maldonado*
Senior Pastor of King Jesus Ministry

If you want to know your identity and find your purpose and fulfill it with the heart of Jesus, this is a must-read book! Alison gives an in-depth look at servanthood and reveals the true heart of a servant. This book will teach you and empower you to live a life that will impact others whether in your family, in your community, in your city, in your nation, and up to the ends of the earth. In a time where the love of many has grown cold, the heart to serve with innocence and purity is desperately needed. This is a book for this generation!

—Pastor Hiubert Zamora
Pastor of King Jesus Ministry

One of the most powerful truths presented in *The Heart of Servanthood* by Minister Alison Marcellus is that every man and woman that has a calling in their life, and God reveals it to them through service. In fact, the level of service is the true measure of building a disciple. Service develops character. It pushes you to live with commitment. It shows us how to be humble; it teaches us how-to walk-in love. It prepares us for our calling, but above all, it reveals God's heart in us, with compassion for His people.

The greatest expression of love is service. This book will really give you insights into what servanthood is and empower you for this season of preparation to your destiny. Minister Alison is not just an amazing teacher, but he truly lives by example. I believe this book is must-read; it will take you to another level of servanthood in your life.

—Evangelist Carlos Licona
Pastor of King Jesus Ministry

Pastor Alison Marcellus has produced a very necessary tool of empowerment for the body of Christ, The Heart of Servanthood. Serving is indeed the pathway to the fulfillment of your destiny. He skillfully pulls hidden truths from God's word to show how this essential principle of serving will cause God's Kingdom to be advance while at the same time, processing you for transformation. Key points such as – Serving is the process God uses to test us before promoting us. Serving is a part of leading because it requires that we hear, direct, and execute. In this self-serving society, we need a constant reminder that serving is indeed the heart of God and the birthing of servanthood in our hearts is necessary as we prepare God's people to reap the end-time harvest and thus usher the second coming of Christ. Service separates the called from the chosen. If you want to be among the chosen and not just the called this is a must read!

Apostle Courtney McLean
Senior Pastor and Founder of Worship and Faith
International Fellowship, Jamaica, W.I.

Preface

The conviction of writing this book came from God. He placed a desire in me to examine the art of servanthood all around me and show readers that everything He creates has a purpose, which becomes a platform to serve from. Nothing that was created or formed by God is purposeless, including *you*. The Bible was created for us to know God and to feed our spirits on the Word of God. The Word is a person, and He wants us to follow His ways, precepts, commandments, and regulations. In Jeremiah 1:5, scripture says, *"Before I formed you in the womb, I knew you; before you were born, I sanctified you. I ordained you a prophet to the nations."* I know that my purpose and calling is to serve people with pastoral care. Even when I did not know I was called to be a pastor, I was always serving people. He put this in me before I was formed in the womb; that's how I automatically recognized the calling. The Bible says, "that all things work together for good and for those that love the Lord" (Romans 8:28). The heart of God is to serve, and if we are made in the image and likeness of God, we should have a heart of servanthood. When we do, our hearts are right.

—Alison Marcellus

Introduction

*T*he beginning of purpose starts with servanthood. The meaning of servanthood is "the role of being a servant." Every purpose has a call to serve. In Acts 20:35, Jesus said it is more blessed to give than to receive. The function of serving is to give, and the characteristics of serving are giving time, energy, and effort. Every man or woman of God, who holds an office in the fivefold ministry serves the church. The objective of a mantle or office of God is to serve people, nations, and humanity. If you don't serve, you cannot lead. To explain it another way, you cannot lead where you haven't served. The essence of a great leader is a person who is in servitude. The Lord took the man Adam and placed him in the garden to cultivate and to keep it (Gen. 2:15). Before God did anything with Adam, he was given responsibility to be the caretaker of the garden. Adam served God by being the landlord of the Eden Estate, which in the book of Genesis, chapter 3, is called the Garden of Eden. Here's another example: it is amazing how Prophet Elijah calls Elisha while he was serving the oxen and working his family business. Elisha was leading his family business and had no idea that God would call him to become a prophet and be Prophet Elijah's successor. Servitude is very important to the Lord God because servitude is part of His mannerism. God never calls lazy people to the servanthood of ministry.

CHAPTER 1

Service Moves the Economy

I want to start this chapter with two stories about the economy. Years ago, in Florida, there was a man who had a big dream. We'll call him Sam. Sam was blessed by God to have a mission of hospitality, and to do it through the Caribbean food he cooked. People felt the love and the nourishment that came through the food he served. Sam then looked around his Florida community and saw that the residents were lacking the unique flavors of Bahamian foods. He opened a restaurant called CG Fish Market and began supplying food and servicing the people of the area with hospitality. Sam's menu included things like conch salad, lobster, shrimp, ceviche fish, fried fish, stewed fish, beans, and rice. The idea caught on with the locals. His restaurant was packed with customers, and he was doing well. It was the feeling of hospitality and the anointing of God on his food that drove people to promote his business by word of mouth. The taste of the food captivated people's taste buds. Sam felt invigorated. Here he was bringing Caribbean vibes to Florida, and people were responding well to its uniqueness.

But all the success led to temptation of the cashiers at the register. Soon it was revealed that money was missing. The number of customers who were dining did not equate to the money in the cash register. There were two types of service occurring at the restaurant—the service Sam

1

was providing and the service that the cashiers were providing to themselves to fill their pocketbooks. Instead of the service increasing the value of the business, this secondary service in the restaurant provoked the actual collapse of the business, and the CG Fish Market had to close. It was months later that Sam realized the mistakes that led up to this business shutdown. Think of what happened to that local economy when the restaurant shut down. Jobs were lost. Friendships between restaurant employees and customers immediately ended. Local taxes were lost. Lost jobs affected families. There were some who went through a rough time because suddenly their mom or dad was not bringing home a check. Single mothers or families were struggling to make ends meet, which was devastating. Similarly, CG Fish Market was no longer going to be a place to take one's date or business group for lunch or dinner. No longer could the customers bathe in the blessing from God that was upon Sam. Sam had the right intention and the "secret sauce" to make the consumers come in and come back. However, someone else's bad service affected his business, removing a good thing in the community. And bad service—or good service—begins with the heart.

Another Story with a Different Ending

Now here is a story that contrasts with CG Fish Market. Dave's restaurant was established in 2006 with Creole and Bahamian dishes. Dave's restaurant is extremely popular among celebrities, such as Dwayne Wade of the Miami Heat, Hollywood actors, and individuals from the music industry. They have a great rapport with him and support his establishment. Unlike cashiers at CG Fish Market, Dave's cashiers give customer service and don't care about servicing their wallets. This allowed Dave to open multiple locations around Miami-Dade County. Now he has a location in the Miami International Airport, Atlanta airport, and in New York City. He has really multiplied himself and become fruitful. Dave's servitude to the community is true and loving; during the pandemic he gave out hundreds of plates of food.

Yearly, Dave gives out bags and school supplies to the kids going back to school and helps youth to overcome literacy problems. Dave's service is to provide food, but he has done more than that. He is a beacon of light and has become the change that transforms the community of Miami-Dade County. The service he provides empowers the community. It made him into a high-profile individual, well-known around the community and high-ranking officials. Being a servant can open doors and take you places you could not imagine before.

Similarities to the Mind of God

Have you ever thought much about how the economy is related to the mind of God?

There are two components that drive the economy: goods and services. *Goods* are the material items that customers are ready to purchase for a price. Goods are tangible items. They can be seen or touched, whereas *services* are intangible items. Goods and services are based on supply and demand. In every part of society, there are services. Servitude is part of our everyday lifestyle that we encounter. It is vital that we understand how important service is in the eternal mind of God. Everything He created—the cosmos, earth, and humanity— was designed with precision to serve in some type of capacity. The sun provides light during the day, which is good for our skin and our immunity. We get plenty of vitamin D from the sun hitting our skin, converting different vitamin D precursors to the vitamin. God made the sun to serve us.

The moon and stars provide light at night. Trees provide humans with oxygen. The clouds produce rain and shade. The ocean or rivers provide an environment for fish. Vehicles serve as transportation for humanity on roadways. A house gives protection and shelter. A job, career, or business provides financial security. These are more examples of how things God made serve us. A bank serves as a financial institution for our money. First responders come to the scene to serve protection, enforce the law, and to aid the public. A hospital serves the sick. Prisons serve those who are rebellious and lawless. A cell phone serves communication verbally, visibly, and gives us the ability to send text messages. These are several examples of how service is built into our lives and how servitude is a lifestyle. Yes, servitude is our lifestyle.

Service from a Natural Stand

Take a breath now and ask yourself, "What is service?" The simple definition of service is something that is intangible, but you can see it in a person and feel it. Services are non-physical, intangible parts of our economy, as opposed to goods that we can touch or handle. Services, such as banking, education, medical treatment, and transportation, make up most of the economies of rich nations. Let's look at the root of the word. The Latin word for service is *slavery*. Slavery is a word that can be very derogatory, delicate, and offensive to anyone. The Latin word here does not mean being in chains or subject to an evil master. Instead, it means being committed and faithful as a servant to someone. It's a bit of a paradigm change, as we must build a new, more positive concept of slavery when it comes to God's Word. There were slaves who were in the Bible, but here we are talking about slaves of God, not slaves of Pharaoh. Read on about how Paul had the grace to be a slave of Christ. Paul wrote a letter in the book of Romans in Romans 1:1 (NLT). He introduced himself as *"a slave of Christ Jesus, chosen by God to be an apostle, sent out to preach His Good News."*

Introducing himself as a slave of Christ, he means he is a willing servant to His ministry and purpose. Apostle Paul says," For we are God's fellow workers" (1 Cor 3:9) ." He has the means to submit—and he does. A synonym for a slave in this instance is a willing fellow laborer, servant, or worker. In the book of Philemon, Onesimus was a worker, or you can say he was a slave to Philemon. This meant he was an employee of Philemon. However, he really wanted to be part of a loving family and to receive brotherly love, which he was not receiving. Most of us have experienced directly or indirectly the mistreatment of ourselves or coworkers who are being disrespected and not valued for their service. That is what Onesimus had to endure from his manager. His solution was to simply run away. Eventually, Onesimus did run away, searching for the brotherly love he wanted. He showed up at the home of Apostle Paul. He told Paul what happened. Apostle Paul wrote Philemon a letter that first acknowledged to Onesimus's boss that he thought of Onesimus as a brother in Christ.

Then Paul asked Philemon to not see Onesimus as a servant, but as someone above the position of a servant—that of a beloved brother. Love doesn't see a slave, but love sees a brother in Christ. Love obeys, submits, and humbles itself before others. Love goes the extra mile to empower others. Paul spoke with Onesimus giving wisdom and understanding the power of forgiveness. I ask that you forgive Philemon as you would myself. Love holds no record of the past; love always forgives." If Onesimus never ran away, Paul would never have met him, nor would he be saved, and correction would not have come to Philemon. Onesimus was mentored by Paul during his stay with Paul, before going back to Philemon he was trained to be a messenger of the gospel of Christ. That is why Paul made the statement "He is no longer a slave to you. He is more than a slave, for he is a beloved brother, especially to me. Now he will mean much more to you, both as a man and as a brother in the Lord". (Philemon 1:16) What happened there became a story that millions of people could learn from in the Bible for hundreds of years to come. Love can be considered a weapon. The greatest legacy to leave on earth is love. Love breaks down walls of culture, religion, tradition, and man's intellectualism. In this story, there was an employee and the employer; but in your life, the relationship might be your marriage, the one between you and your children, or family struggles you are dealing with that address a lack of love and acceptance. This is a story, but it also may be your reality.

A Company's Force Is Servility

The strength of a company is determined by its ability to serve. Once service is a strong drive in the company, that company is a force to reckon with! Therefore, all great companies have great customer service. You encounter their servitude before you even get the product or goods you wanted to purchase. Every entity that provides service for you can enhance your business or bankrupt your business—and it happens by word of mouth. The greatest serviceability in today's market is Chick-Fil-A. They are in the fast-food industry. Do you have one near you? My opinion Chick-Fil-A has the best customer care out of any industry I have experienced by far; no other company or industry comes close, not even any hospital, airport, restaurant, leasing office, car dealership, supermarket, or school district—you get my point. As a customer, you're valued and honored more than the money in your wallet. For example, Chick-Fil-A services have a few characteristics they display.

Whatever state, city, or county you go to that has a Chick-Fil-A, you will experience politeness, hospitality, caring, an assuring attitude, and attentive employees who are friendly, kind, and committed to provide excellent care of you as the customer. They never see you as a dollar bringer. They never miss seeing *you,* and you are not treated as invisible. Their service connects to your heart, and you commit your money and time to them. You want to experience their vision. They are a company that follows Christian principles, and what they are doing is a strong example of how Christ would want the world to experience Him. Chick-Fil-A employees administer unforgettable, real evidence of kingdom service. There are a lot of videos on social media displaying how greats Chick-Fil-A service are. Why don't we see this type of service more often in other establishments? What makes society immune to bad service? Why is bad service the norm? Where did that start, and who started it?

Rejection of Servitude

Let's go to Revelation 12:7–9 (KJV) for a moment:

And there was war in heaven: Michael and his angels fought against the dragon, and his angels, and fought and his angels, and prevailed not; neither was their place found any more in heaven. And the great dragon was cast out, that old serpent, called the devil, and Satan, which he was cast out into the earth and his angels were cast out with him." "Yes, he told them I saw Satan fall from heaven like lightning. (Luke 10:18 NLT)

Once Lucifer went against the will of God, he wasn't Lucifer anymore. He became Satan. Lucifer fell from his position once he abandoned his post of serving. God created a cherub Lucifer, called the angel of light. Once pride kicked in, Lucifer began thinking he was equal to God. Lucifer rejected what God called him to be. He tried convincing other angels to overthrow God and was then overthrown himself. That's when his name was changed to Satan. Scripture also calls Lucifer a dragon, or Satan, the one deceives the whole world. He was thrown down to the earth with all his angel followers. We see how Satan was evicted out of heaven. Heaven is an atmosphere of peace and glory, but Satan violated heaven's protocol by provoking a war against God. He fell from heaven like lightning, according to (Luke 10:18).

The Concept of Process

I use the term *process* in this book a lot. What do I mean by process? The definition of process is a natural phenomenon marked by gradual changes that lead toward a particular result, a continuing natural or biological activity or function, or a series of actions or operations continuing to an end Merriam-Webster. A process is a continuous series of actions, steps, and changes that lead to a result or destination. We go through a process spiritually so we can be transformed. Here are a couple of examples of processes in different areas of life. The process for humanity to reproduce includes a woman becoming pregnant and the baby maturing to full term in nine months. Now if the baby is born before nine months, that child is considered premature. The process time for the baby to be fully matured is the full nine months. The financial advisor of Shaquille O'Neal processed him financially with wisdom. We know this because he does not use his contract money from the NBA. He lives off his endorsement money. Most athletes spend their money from their base contract, but he does not because he has been processed financially with wisdom. The education process is that you go from elementary to middle school to high school and then to college. Just about everything in our life comes down to a process.

The process allows us to grow. How long is the process of perfection? Lucifer submitted himself to God, but the Bible never tells us how long. In eternity, time does not exist. In the book of Ezekiel 28:13–15 (NKJV), scripture says this:

> "You were in Eden, the garden of God. Every precious stone was your covering, the sardius, topaz, and diamond, beryl, onyx, and jasper, sapphire, turquoise, and emerald with gold. The workmanship of your timbrels and pipes was prepared for you on the day you were created. You were the anointed cherub who covers; I established you; You were on the holy mountain of God; you walked back and forth in the midst of fiery stones. You were perfect in your ways from the day you were created, till iniquity was found in you."

Perfection is the quality or state of being perfect, such as freedom from fault or defect: flawlessness, maturity; the state of being saintly, and exemplification of supreme excellence. It's also the act or process of perfecting. He was created in perfection. Everything God made was created to serve from perfection. Lucifer became familiar with God and thought within himself that he could be like God.

Familiarity is defined in the dictionary as a good knowledge of something, or the fact that you know something so well Cambridge English Dictionary. And a state of close relationship Merriam-Webster. Lucifer was the first one of all God's "thoughts in motion" to reject the heavenly Father in the place of servanthood. Lucifer was an angel who serviced the throne of God with worship. He was created to lead worship day and night before the holy presence of God. In the book of Ezekiel, we learn that iniquity evicted Lucifer from heaven. The purpose of God's production (creation) is immaculate. A car manufacturer has production that requires different types of cars to be produced for the public. In the same way, the production of God is His creation, whatever He created. In the book of Genesis, His creation was in full display as the moon, sun, trees, oceans, stars, animals, humans, and much more. But let's get back to explaining more about a "thought in motion." In the mind of God, everything was made with the intent of maturity and full-ness. A baby is dependent, but in the mind of God, He sees an adult. The caterpillar is the beginning of a butterfly; God always saw the butterfly.

The thought in motion is seeing beyond what is being seen. Isaiah 46:10 (ESV) reinforces this idea with the words, *"declaring the end from the beginning and from ancient times things not yet done, saying, my counsel shall stand, and I will accomplish all my purpose"*. This brings up Satan's iniquity (Ezek. 28:15 Amp) *"You were perfect in your ways from the day you were created, till iniquity was found in you."* What is iniquity? Etymologically, iniquity means "twisted and distorted." It is anything that turns away from God's original intent and perfect path. Satan abandoned, rejected, and disowned his calling, purpose, and des-tiny to fulfill his own agenda. Everything was conceived to serve God directly or indirectly. Now Satan serves himself, being self-centered, self-righteous, self-seeking, self-indulgent, selfish, egotistical, full of self, and prideful. In other words, he is all self-willed. The name *Satan* means a grand adversary of man; the devil or prince of darkness; the chief of the fallen angels and the one who resists. In the King James Version (KJV) dictionary, Satan is the founder of independence, which means he serves himself. He sets a cadence to himself. Independence is one of the attributes of an individual who does not care nor has the heart to serve; it identifies their god by their actions.

So, if your service is independent of the service God wants you to do, you start to become like Satan. You start serving yourself. You are the likeness of Satan's characteristics. These are the fruits of the flesh that are in alliance with darkness according to Galatians 5:19–21 (KJV)

> *Now the works of the flesh are manifest, which are these; Adultery, fornication, uncleanness, lasciviousness, idolatry, witchcraft, hatred, variance, emulations, wrath, strife, seditions, heresies, envying's, murders, drunkenness, retellings, and such like of the which I tell you before, as I have also told you in time past, that they which do such things shall not inherit the kingdom of God.*

The devil knows that if you are engaged in any of his entrapments, you are disqualified from inheriting the kingdom of God. The great apostle Paul mentioned these are all the attributes of spoiled fruit, manifested by the way of the flesh. There are many ways to serve on this planet, laboring in darkness or light. The verse in Galatians above shows what side your work is rendered to. You do not need a revelation for that. Service allows transformation in the heart. The minute you stop serving, you become stagnant in your salvation, also your actions are saying to God that His eternal purpose and plans for your life are not good enough.

The thoughts you think of yourself are much greater than what God thinks of you. At that point, you become an enemy to God. You become like the prophet Jonah, who didn't want to follow God's instructions. He was like a little child, having a tantrum in the grocery store. Jonah wouldn't even talk to God about what he was thinking and feeling. He was self-willed and ended up dying in his self-will even though he was a prophet. Do you see some similarities to Lucifer here? There are five things I will highlight when speaking of service. Each of these will be a blessing to your life and open your eyes to the importance of serving in your church in my opinion, family, business, marriage, friendship, and any areas of life. In your servanthood, you will be processed, promoted, pruned, humbled, and transformed in your heart. Let us begin this journey and watch where the Holy Spirit will take us.

Summary

Servanthood is not a topic that ignites the church, but it is the topic that builds those areas mentioned above and generates a solid foundation of Christ-like character in the body of Christ. And once you have that, you attract others who want to be like you (and thus like Christ).

Prayer

Heavenly Father, I come before your presence and submit my life to You. I repent for my rejection of servitude and not submitting to the will of God. I ask for forgiveness under the blood of Jesus Christ. Cleanse me with the blood of Jesus; also, I commit to allowing my heart to be changed and transformed. Give me the grace and revelation of servanthood. I submit my service of gifts, talents, anointings, and body to the kingdom of God. To be led, directed, and guided by You Holy Spirit. Father, thank you for your grace and love to serve you. Amen.

CHAPTER 2

God's Way of Process is Through Service

*T*he supernatural, the power of God, the glory of God, healing, deliverance, prophesying, and the word of knowledge: all these are God's abilities that are manifested through his servants. Many men and women are excited to be used by the Lord in a magnificent and tremendous way. These abilities are what make people stand out and separate them from the multitude, showing that there is a special grace of God upon that individual's life. The public demonstration of the talents and giftings from God is what people see. The longevity of their service does not come naturally. A ministry can get cut off if they don't do what God requires.

The talents and gifts from God—the anointing—is based on five things:

1. Commitment
2. Responsibility
3. Loyalty
4. Love
5. Faithfulness

Five Things That Bring in the Supernatural

Let's look at all five of these factors, define them, and discuss their importance.

Commitment

Commitment is "an agreement or pledge to do something in the future, an engagement to assume a financial obligation at a future date, something pledged, and "an act of committing to a charge or trust: such as an act of referring a matter to a legislative committee."–Merriam-Webster Dictionary Commitment is the foundation of any relationship in a healthy life. It involves dedicating yourself to something, a person, or a cause. Commitment obligates you to do something. The best way to describe commitment and make it visible to your imagination is with the example of marriage. In a marriage, there is a vow between both parties that states this contract is for a lifetime. The longevity of the agreement is part of the vow, so you have the idea "to have and to hold from this day forward, for better, for worse, for richer, for poorer, for sickness, and in health, to love and to cherish, till death do us part." The "till death do us part" can't get more definite on the longevity of the vow. These words show us that challenges will arise. You will, no doubt, be blindsided by a trial at one time or another, and surprising circumstances will occur. Commitment withstands all weaknesses, insecurities, and disadvantages.

Commitment is not a race. It is a marathon. When things are going well, you will never be confronted with challenges to commitment. But when things become ugly or uncomfortable, that's when commitment becomes crucial. Only in adverse situations is commitment validated, expressed, challenged, or reaffirmed. When you're committed in difficult situations, there's a revelation of yourself. Yes, that's right—how you act when things get tough brings out your real character. But how can commitment become a lifestyle in your life? The answer is in the renewing of the mind, mentioned in Romans 12:2. *"And be not conformed to this world; but be transformed by the renewing of your mind, that you may prove what is that good, acceptable, and perfect will of God."*

The only way for you to identify what is the acceptable, good, and perfect will of God is the transformation of your mind; shifting and being renewed is by not conforming to this world.

If you conform to the world, you will not see the acceptable, good, and the perfect will of God before your face, whether it's in business, relationships, ministry, or an opportunity sent by God. Simply, you won't be able to discern it even if it's right in front of you. Adam was given a task by God. He and Eve could not eat from a certain tree in the Garden of Eden. The righteousness of God is a law, which provides boundaries and restrictions for our benefits. Yet they both did exactly what they should not have done. They had been confronted by the wickedest being on the earth. Satan had no authority at that time. Adam and Eve were not committed to the divine instructions given to them by the Author of all creation. Therefore, because their minds were not committed to God, Adam and Eve were unable to follow directions. Eve obeyed the voice of the serpent and ate the fruit from the forbidden tree, then she gave the fruit to her husband. Adam ate from the tree of sin, and Jesus Christ came to die on the tree, which provided the forgiveness of sin.

For Jesus, His mission was "to destroy the works of the enemy" (1 John 3:8). The "beautiful" things Jesus did were the miracles, signs, deliverance, resurrecting the dead, healings, and the supernatural becoming natural. His total commitment and focus were the cross and the agreement He had made with the Father in heaven. (Revelation 13:8) NLT says: *"the lamb was slain before the world was made"* . Jesus never lost focus on His mission; He was constantly reminding his disciples of his upcoming death. More importantly, He spoke and prophesied about the cross, calling it into his imagination. The cross was a sign of commitment; Jesus was committed to destroying the works of (Satan in nature) sin.

Responsibility

Responsibility is the state or fact of having a duty to deal with something or having control (as a parent, caregiver, or power of attorney (POA) over someone. Responsibility gives you a duty you must complete, and it's something you are meant to do. Every title in life has a responsibility. It does not matter what position you have: parent, athlete, supervisor, president, student, pastor, janitor, or in marriage. Responsibility is instruction or direction to fulfill an obligation to a person, place, or thing. God calls us to be responsible for many different things. For example, we are first responsible for our body; the body is called a temple, house, and a dwelling place for the Spirit of God to rest. We must be good stewards of our health and spiritual life. (1 Corinthians) 6:19) NIV states: *"Do you not know that your bodies are temples of the Holy Spirit, who is in you, whom you have received from God? You are not your own."*

Health demands us not to open a door for the enemy to attack us. Yet how many of us are irresponsible with our eating habits? If we eat junk food, our body will become a junkyard for sicknesses, diseases, and illnesses. All three of these—heart disease, high blood pressure, and diabetes—are the fruits of bad eating, and they give rights to the enemy to abide, attack, and become a resident in your body. Your spiritual responsibilities are to live a clean, pure, and consecrated lifestyle as a Christian in holiness. Matthew 6:33 states: *"Seek first the kingdom of God and his righteousness and all things will be added to you."* To find the kingdom of God requires a pursuit of intimacy, building a close relationship in these various of ways: reading the Bible, praying, fasting, worshiping, praising, and meditating on God relentlessly are what we are called to do. When you do them, your mind isn't allowed to have appetites, cravings, and desires for worldly things. That's because they occupy your mind and thoughts with spiritual matters and spiritual activities. In doing these activities, you realize it is your priestly responsibility, and you are committed to the Holy Spirit so the Father's glory can manifest and become a natural essence in your life.

Loyalty

Loyalty is the state of being loyal. Loyalty is being committed whether things are going well or not great. Loyalty is a sign of love, and it has a vow to not quit. This beautiful characteristic is birthed out of being a servant of God. When dealing with people, even in the house of God, you will get treated like a rug that lost all its fluffiness. What do I mean by this? Some of the most rebellious people are in the church. I served as an usher a few times. I have witnessed and experienced disobedience while leading, directing, and guiding the people to bring order in the house of God. Jesus was praised as he entered Jerusalem in John 12:13 (KJV): *"Hosanna blessed is the king of Israel that comes in the name of the Lord."* A week later, the same group of people shouted to crucify and kill him, as recorded in John 19:12. If this can happen to Jesus, then we cannot expect anything different for our own life. Despite the people chanting with a vehement attitude toward Christ Jesus, He never lost His loyalty to the cross and to the Father. He expected to experience an encounter of torture, pain, bruising, beating, disfigurement, and death. You will never know how loyal a person is until they are under pressure. The pressure is what reveals the true state of the person's heart.

Love

Love is the essence of giving. Love is a characteristic of serving. Love is not stingy, mean, selfish, or evil; love constantly lives in a state of courtesy. Love cannot be counterfeit, fabricated, or fictitiously illustrated; if it was, it would be seen as non-organic, fake. Love overcomes virtually everything that comes before it. The Bible says that love covers a multitude of sins (1 Peter 4:8). Love covers you so you are not full of shame, guilt, and regret. You serve others out of the abundance of the heart, not from your head. Love is seen, felt, and heard. In servanthood, love is the essential pillar that is exposed. In the times we are living in, one of the essential work fields that is constantly reported on the media circuit is the police. This new decade of 2020 has been a time where policemen have demonstrated brutality caught on phone cameras around the country. The function of the heart of the first responder is to de-escalate and resolve a situation so everyone is treated righteously. Most police incidents have shown that they have a heart of stone that is being seen. Love does not discriminate. Love is not prejudiced or racist and does not condone racism. Love multiplies, love increases, love influences, and love leaves a legacy as Jesus did with His death on the cross.

Love is always interjecting peace, unity, and comfort; in the time of this pandemic crisis in the world, the heart is manifested with lack of love showing hate, division, and anger. The Bible says that in the last days, men's hearts will wax cold (Matt 24:12). This means love will be nonexistent and society's heart will be like a rock when it comes to evil intent. In the 1950s and 1960s, Martin Luther King Jr. stood for peace. All he wanted was equality among African Americans and White Americans. Martin Luther King, Jr. spearheaded the Civil Rights Movement and led large groups of people, marching peacefully with no intent to fight, riot, or cause a disturbance. The heart of some White Americans was full of anger, hate, and malice towards the African Americans; they would violently attack, spit, hit, and curse them. Even the hearts of the children waxed cold, expressing vulgar and discriminating words like the adults. The Bible says, "out of the abundance of the heart the mouth speaks" in (Luke 6:45b) NKJV. The fruit of the heart are words that are uttered, that also describe the condition of the heart. Even when they would release dogs to bite them, Martin Luther King Jr. still would walk in love and not hate, prophesying to the future, "I have a dream that little Black boys and girls will be holding hands with little White boys and girls." His dream was the manifestation of love unity. God showed him the future in the worse of time; in which some blacks and whites would have never imagine we are living what he saw and spoke.

Love declares unity and togetherness. Love is joy and righteous. Love will endure to the end and prevail in victory. How you serve people in society is the reflection of your heart. Respect and honor are attracted out of love. When you serve from love; people become blessed as you serve, and appreciation is born. Adam and Eve were given a simple command by the Father to not eat from the Tree of the Knowledge of Good and Evil. It's Satan who will always tell you who you are not. When you believe it, he takes you out of the place of identity with the Lord where authority is established. Thus, you end up relinquishing your position to Satan due to disobedience. Genesis 3:5b states: *"And you shall be as gods, knowing good and evil."* They were already appointed by God Almighty to rule over the garden and maintain it. The decree was made by God Himself--anything that is made a law on earth must first be declared in the realm of the spirit to legislate that ordinance. After a conversation, Eve was intrigued by the dialog. It was sweet to her ears. Adam just watched and gave into eating the fruit, which they were ordered not to eat. Genesis 3:6 (NLT) tells the story that the woman was convinced. She saw that the tree was beautiful, its fruit looked delicious, and she wanted the wisdom it would give her. So, she took some of the fruit and ate it.

Then she gave some to her husband, who was with her, and he ate it too. There are ways to observe and understand the world around us. There are five main ways we can do this: through sight (with our eyes), touch (with our fingers), smell (with our nose), taste (with our tongue) and hearing (with our ears). The natural senses of Eve caused sin to paralyze humanity. Eve was enticed by her five senses: (1) she listened to the serpent; (2) she looked at the fruit; (3) she touched the fruit; and (4) she ate the fruit; and (5) smell of the fruit. All five senses were used to assist with treason in the garden. Our natural senses work the same way in the spiritual realm.

Faithfulness

Faithfulness means being steadfast in affection or allegiance and being firm in adherence to promises or in observance of duty, given with strong assurance, binding a faithful promise. Jesus was the second Adam, sent to make amends for the first Adam (1 Cor 15:45-47). Since Adam gave over authority by eating from the tree, Jesus had to die on the tree to retrieve the authority that was hijacked through treason. One of God's words to his children is Hebrews 13:5. *"I would never leave thee nor forsake thee."* Zephaniah 3:17 states, *"The Lord thy God in the midst of thee is mighty; He will save, He will rejoice over thee with joy; He will rest in His love, He will joy over thee with singing."* The grace of God is His faithfulness. Every day you see grace, He has been faithful. Jesus was faithful to these things: to the Word that governed His walk, His relationship with Abba Father, and through the betrayals, agony, and sufferings to the cross. Nothing that came to oppose His faithfulness distracted Him from His purpose. Jesus never allowed anything to be a distraction. His focus was kept on the mission to regain the keys from the enemy. Having a target set before you keep you faithful to the mission ahead.

Path to Promotion

A young shepherd boy in Bethlehem attended his father's sheep in the backside of the desert, a place where none of his other siblings wanted to take that responsibility. Imagine smelling the raw stench of urine from the sheep and the fragrance of manure. The young man's name was David, and he loved the chore that was bestowed upon him. He was accountable for all the sheep. None of them went missing from sunrise to sunset, day in and day out. His commitment to those sheep as a shepherd boy, and constant heed to the instruction and obligation of his duty, was displayed in 1 Samuel 17:34: *'And David said to King Saul, 'Thy servant kept his father's sheep, and came a lion and a bear, and took a lamb out of the flock. And I went out after him and delivered it out of his mouth; and when he arose against me, I caught him by the beard, and smote him, and slew him."* Those words were said with such passion and faith in his ability to do it again. There was no one there with David at the time. He was not trying to manipulate his father or brothers. He was unlike many people in the church--ones who serve with a bad heart and in an atmosphere of darkness.

David did not have to cut a person low with lies, compromise values, backbite, discredit, or devalue another's character or work ethic for a position or a title. David was the manager of the family business. His responsibility was to take charge of the family economy. He served with an authentic heart in his servanthood. His faithfulness, loyalty, and trustworthiness caught the eye of God Almighty. While David was doing all this behind the scenes, his older siblings were in the king's army. They were all bigger, stronger, and better looking, but they all lacked one thing. What David had was the heart of a warrior and a love for God. At this same time, God had already ousted King Saul from his kingly role and assignment to Israel. In the Old Testament, a king was identical to an apostle in the New Testament. Both ruled and reigned from a position of authority to legislate and to enforce decrees and commands. Look at 1 Samuel 16:10. We see that Jesse brought all seven of his sons before the prophet. Both he and the prophet Samuel separately had the thought that one of the young men would be the choice of God. In verse 10, Jesse admits to having another son in the backside of the desert. In the prophetic mind of God, David was in the background while everyone else was waiting with the prophet for his appearance. Naturally, he is in the back, but spiritually he is in front of the priest and leader of the family.

It is so much like God to never pick the person that is the best looking, more talented, the one that everyone would choose, or pick someone from the best neighborhood. *"The last shall be first and the first shall be last" (Matt 20:16)* is what we see within the scriptural story of David and his brothers. The oil would not flow for the other seven brothers, but in 1 Samuel 16:13, as David sat down, the oil began to flow and gushed out upon his body. The anointing and the spirit of God had come upon him. Our Father is a God of numbers. David was the eighth child, and that number means resurrection, a new beginning, and new order or creation. David was promoted and became the new king of Israel in front of his father and brothers; they had no idea. God released supernatural grace within his spirit to lead a nation. As we serve God, He will release the promotion. It doesn't matter where you are in life; God will send someone to you for your commitment to serving in the kingdom of God. This is a kingdom principle of how you can accelerate your promotion in your life by rendering service to God.

Prophet Samuel was promoted to be the mouthpiece of God to Israel. Samuel's mother left him with the priest named Eli. Samuel's responsibility was to serve Eli as a student. God never does anything without a purpose, and His ways are greater than our ways and His thoughts are higher than our thoughts (Isaiah 55:9). As a little boy, Samuel became the bridge between God and Eli, the priest of Israel. In serving, Samuel learned to lead because God was changing the guards of Israel, and the prophet would become the voice of God to the people. Not only that, but he would be the voice of God that was always accurate. The servanthood of Samuel guaranteed none of his words as a prophet would fall short of the truth.

Death to Self

The world is dead spiritually because of sin; the sin of the world is naturally bound. There are two realms: the natural and the spiritual. The devil is supernaturally in darkness. Sin handicaps us to the natural realm of living. The devil knows that if you sin, you could never fight him; sin empowers the devil to have rights in the life of man.

If you are not dead to your flesh, you will mature in sin. In Acts 2:1, the Holy Spirit came to serve and to empower the body of Christ, giving them the ability to serve within the kingdom of God on earth. If you do not go to your own funeral, figuratively speaking, you will never see the greatness that God deposited when He created you. What do I mean by going to your own funeral? Death to self is living a life of holiness, righteousness, consecration, purification, and sanctification. Death to self is the ability to resist the devil and reject all temptation from the devil. James 4:7–8 (ESV) states: "*Submit yourself before God. Resist the devil and he will flee. Draw near to God and God will draw near to you.*" Resisting the devil begins with submitting yourself to the Lord Jesus, giving him all access to be Lord in every area of your life: mentally, emotionally, spiritually, physically, and financially. There are things you cannot get from God with confession, as you can with death to self or dying to self. Your death is the entrance to greatness on the inside of you. People go to seminars for the ability to master different habits, traits, and characteristics. First Corinthians 9:27 (NLT) says: "*I discipline my body like an athlete, training it to do what it should. Otherwise, I fear that after preaching to others I myself might be disqualified.*"

Until you can master your flesh's perverseness, then corrupted motives, evil ways, habits, and agendas will be part of your character. The Bible says in Romans 6:23, "*For the wages of sin is death.*" Death is earned through an accumulation of sin; the maturity of sin is death. Sin is accomplished with the flesh. If you are dead to the flesh, sin has no grounds to manifest. If you're not dead to the flesh, you mature in sin. You cannot love people until you serve people. When you serve people, you're an expression of God's genuine love. You must die to self each day. Unless you die to the fullness of self, you will always be selfish. When you see people get blessed and serve them, it is such a joyful time. But selfishness is not joyful; it's depressing. Look for a minute at Galatians 2:20: "*When you are serving, you are giving of yourself; but when you do not serve, you are saving yourself to yourself, there is no satisfaction in being self-centered, self-righteous, self-seeking, self-interested, mean, and stingy.*"

One thing that you realize in serving in any capacity in the house of God is the death of the flesh. The flesh is the first thing that must die.

The flesh is anti-Christ and always active to undermine the things of the spirit. The flesh does not want to be under submission to anyone or to follow rules and regulations. As we serve the Lord within the body of Christ, we die to self, which requires us to be under authority. Death is the only way to increase with God; it is amazing that natural death takes us into another dimension or realm in the spirit. Similarly, in dying to self, we enter another sphere of influence or level in the Holy Ghost. Death to self brings new speed, new levels, a new dimension, new realms, new fire, and new passion; the newness of God comes by way of death to self. Dying demands an increase of God. James 4:7–8 (KJV) states this: *Submit yourselves therefore to God. Resist the devil, and he will flee from you. Draw nigh to God, and he will draw nigh to you. Cleanse your hands, ye sinners; and purify your hearts, ye double minded.*

Submitting and resisting is a sign that the flesh is dead because the flesh is corruptive and disobedient. We see in verse 8 that it begins with drawing nigh to God, which is denying self and attracts God to be closer to you. God hates sin, so if you are drawing near to him, sin is not a lifestyle anymore. Death to self draws God's attention to increase, deposit, and impart more of Himself in us. Servanthood requires a funeral; without it, we would not be able to serve the Lord. We can attend church services but never do anything to help the church in any capacity. Many people come to a church service, expecting something, and complaining about what is not right or what is wrong, but never make the effort to assist with enhancing the house of the Lord. By submitting yourself to God, you resist the devil; the flesh is bound once you align to the things of God.

Servanthood Reveals You to You

There are many people who are confused, discouraged, and frustrated because they don't know what their purpose is in life. One of the fruits of confusion and frustration is suicide. Not having surety causes the mind to be in a tormented state, which is a lack of peace. Most people I have known that dealt with suicide say the same thing––they all felt empty and had no reason to live because they had no purpose. As simple as peace may sound, it's often not taken seriously. Without peace, you will find yourself mentally unhealthy. When you are far from God and not in a relationship with Him, any one of the mental disorders—depression, anxiety, stress, or fear—could become your reality. We all face stress, but we don't live in it. These emotions should not be a life-style. You will face challenges and might have a temporary time to feel depression. But the Holy Spirit will guide you and instruct you to pray until it passes. These feelings are not our long-term state when we live in Him. Seeking the kingdom is by praying, worshiping, praising, and declaring the Word of God to God. The ultimate purpose for seeking the kingdom of God is to be in His presence and glory.

Success in life lies in asking yourself questions and answering them. Everyone usually asks themselves four questions before maturing into the fullness of His calling. All these questions begin with a mysterious letter "W":

1. Who am I?
2. Why was I born?
3. Where did I come from?
4. What is my purpose??

The word says this in Matthew 22:14 (KJV) *"For many are called, but few are chosen."* Everyone is called to something, but you will not find the call unless you serve God. In the spirit, God made man, and in the natural, He formed man. The creation of man was in the Spirit years before time was in existence; we were and still are spirit beings. Every human has a spirit, yet we all are wearing an earth suit. The suit is flesh from the dust of the earth. God spoke to, interacted with, and had fellowship and communion with you and me in heaven. Jeremiah 1:5 (NKJV) teaches us this: *"Before I formed you in the womb I knew you, and before you were born I ordained you a prophet to the nations."*

When we are born as babies, we learn a totally new culture. It is not a kingdom culture, nor is it to fear the Lord. All of us lose our sense of who God was in our lives when we become a human being. We forget what it was like when we were spirit beings in heaven. Once you receive Jesus into your heart (salvation), you can get the inner knowing that God is a Father. It might come sooner or later to you.

Some people can't see God as a Father because they had an abusive father in real life, and it takes them a while to get the inner knowing. You don't learn that God is your Father in your mind; it's an inner knowing, there has to be a revelation. Jesus came to reveal the heart of the Father to this generation. Therefore, Jesus tells us I only do what my Father says or does (John 5:19). He's telling us that we should do the same thing. Jesus is emphasizing relationship and intimacy with the Father. Jesus never called the father God. The strong concordance the meaning of father in Greek is pater; begetter, originator, progenitor- one in "intimate connection and relationship". When someone says father immediately it states relationship, connection, and intimacy. Jesus says in (Matt 6:10) pray Our Father, in the Merriam-Webster father is source where we receive from. Our spirit connects, retrieves, and remembers; it might not be fully recovered, but it has a revelation God is real and that we were with Him in eternity. That type of knowledge is revealed in the heart of man.

Familiarity Births Spiritual Death

Lucifer is the father of familiarity. He wanted to become like God to overthrow His kingdom by way of envy, jealousy, competition, independence, and manipulating a few angels along the way. Those are a few traits the spirit of familiarity harvests within the heart of a person. The definition of familiarity is close acquaintance with or knowledge of something; a feeling of comfort or closeness with someone. Familiarity is kind of odd in that a diamond would become common to someone who has the eyes of familiarity. In the Bible, there are many different people that were familiar either with God, their gift, or the leader God chose. God chose Moses to lead the people out of Egypt, delivering them from the captivity of Pharaoh. By the grace of God, they lived in the wilderness for forty years. Through it all, God spoke to Moses and gave him instructions, directions, revelation, and regulations to govern the Israelites. Miriam and Aaron were siblings of Moses, and in the book of Numbers chapter 12, they began to speak against Moses saying, *"the Lord did not only speak with Moses but also to us."* They were upset because Moses married an Ethiopian.

The Lord heard what they were saying about Moses. He came down and visited them in front of Moses. God confronted Aaron and Miriam and cursed her with leprosy; half of her flesh was eaten away. Miriam and Aaron had brought their relationship with Moses into the familiar realm. They did not see him as a man who hears from God and lost the respect and conviction of their brother's mantle. He had already led over two million people out of Egypt and through the desert. The whole time he had been directed by God. Familiarity is a death sentence to your spiritual life. Korah, Dathan, and Abriam were men of different tribes, who challenged and opposed Moses. In 1 Samuel 15:23a (NKJV), scripture says, *"For rebellion is as the sin of witchcraft and stubbornness is as iniquity and idolatry."* Those three men also took part in melting the gold to create a golden calf as a god. Egypt was infested with the works of the occult. The great Pharaoh was feared by countries nearby because of his occultist ways. The three men wanted to challenge Moses, but they were opposing God.

There were 250 of them in total. Besides Korah, Dathan, and Abriam, there were others who joined them, including their families and other men. Fierce fire came from God that opened the ground and swallowed them alive with their belongings. Then the ground closed back together as though nothing happened (Numbers 16:16-35). You must guard your heart above all else and examine your heart daily that there is no mixture in you. Are you familiar with your spouse, parents, children, and pastor? The prophet Jonah was sent to release the decree of the Lord to

Nineveh, with one condition: if they repented, He would have mercy on them and the land. God was not pleased and decided to bring judgment; but the people of Nineveh believed God, proclaimed a fast, and put on sackcloth, from the greatest of them to the least of them Jonah 3:5. The people of Nineveh were Gentiles. They were not Jewish, did not know God, and did not have a relationship with Him. They heard of God's manifestation and power with the neighboring countries.

Even the king of Nineveh cried mightily to God; man, and beast did the same. That pleased the Lord, and He repented of what He said and did not do it. The heart of Prophet Jonah reflects Nineveh, the wicked nation. Nineveh was the nation he was sent to judge. Jonah was familiar with God. Every time God sent Jonah to a nation, the nation would repent. Jonah didn't want Nineveh to repent. If they turned from their wicked ways, they wouldn't get judged. God's will was not good enough for the prophet. Jonah revealed the agenda in his heart. He was the voice of God but did not have the heart of God. His heart was so hardened, he himself ran from the presence of God. The will of Jonah and the presence of God were not synchronized. Jonah was so angry with God that he ignored Elohim, which caused him to become independent of God. Familiarity is a sign of immaturity, a man with an immature heart die of premature death. The disrespect and dishonor to God was birthed by being familiar with God; Jonah died in the state of anger with a hardened heart.

Honor and Humility

Exodus 20:12 (NKJV) states: *Honor your father and your mother, that your days may be long in the land that the Lord your God is giving you.* The Word says to honor your mother and father so that your days will be long upon the land which the Lord your God gives you. When we honor our parents, we do not get familiar with them. We have all been in the mall, plaza, or grocery store, and have seen kids scream, curse, yell, fight, and disrespect their parents. This is a sign of familiarity, one that removes the respect level between children and parents. The scripture is telling us to serve our parents with respect and honor, not to see them as equals but, instead, have reverence toward them. There will always be a progression from one generation to another. Even if your parents were illiterate and you went to college and got a degree, one should always respect your parents. Familiarity blinds parents to not see their kids like God does. One example is Jesse as a father. He never saw his son as a king, only as a shepherd boy who was looking after the family business. If you are a parent, are you familiar with your children, or do you see them the way God sees them?

Testimony of Familiarity

Familiarity is a sign of comfort and with it, there is no longer reverence or esteem. My friend's mom named Sally was attending a doctor's office for years. As Sally came in for periodic visits, the doctor learned more about the patient's children and family. She conversed with Sally and did the required tests. After a while, Sally went on a diet and lost weight. However, her stomach was increasing in size. Her doctor said nothing about it. Sally decided to change physicians. Since she was a new patient, the new doctor did an extensive examination and blood work looking at the results and all her vitals in her body carefully. Test results came back with a diagnosis of fibroids on her ovaries. This was a serious matter because it could lead to many other problems. Immediately they scheduled a procedure to remove the fibroids. Familiarity could have caused her health to be compromised had she not pursued a new doctor. At her first doctor's office, familiarity was leading her to health problems. But with the new doctor, there was a resurrected assurance of health.

Prayer

Father God, I recognize that I have grieved and quenched the Holy Spirit. I repent of my sin of disobedience, rebellion, and familiarity. I repent for not allowing the process to take place in my heart. I ask for forgiveness and surrender all my being to You, Lord Jesus. I pray for the grace of God through the blood of Jesus Christ to die to self, die to my will, die to my emotions, and to crucify to my flesh. May the grace of the Holy Spirit empower me in my servanthood that will release benefits of promotion, increase, revelation, wisdom, honor, humility and more of God's presence in my life. I pray that in my servanthood, I am committed, responsible, loyal, faithful, in my walk to love people. Amen.

CHAPTER 3

Service Separates the Called and the Chosen

*M*any want to know the answer to the question, what is my purpose? What was I created to do? What is the calling for my life? All through the scriptures, men/women served before their calling was revealed and before they were anointed for their purpose. Some examples were Jacob, Daniel, Zachariah, Esther, and Ruth, but I want to focus on the story of Rahab the harlot. Serving are the process God uses to test, examine, and search our hearts to develop maturity in us. As infants, we were served with milk, given baths, and clothed by our parents. Our hearts became full of self because we were receiving without giving. We became selfish and not selfless. I like the story of Rahab, the harlot in Jericho. Her story invokes lust, perversion, seduction, and solicitation of all the men of the city with sexual activities. With this type of occupation, the choices for where she lived were restricted to a zone at the back wall of the city. Rahab and the entire city of Jericho heard of God's supernatural signs and wonders, including when God opened a way for the Israelites in the Red Sea, making a passageway so His people could escape. They probably cringed when they heard about Moses defeating the great pharaoh in Egypt and then the defeat of the two Amonite kings. The supernatural intervention no doubt ignited fear throughout all of Jericho toward the God of the Israelites.

The king of Jericho got word that Rahab had some Israelites in her home. Guards were sent to her immediately, but she hid the "spies" on her roof. She served the men and made a covenant with them that she would help them. She told them she had heard about the power of their God. Rahab made a covenant with the Israelite spies that when they came back to Jericho, her family would be saved. Rahab had no idea she was walking in her calling by serving the spies; then she became part of the lineage of Jesus Christ. Rahab's service gave her an opportunity to intermingle with the Israelites. She married Salmon and became the mother of Boaz, who became a wealthy man in Bethlehem. Rahab had a revelation and her *kairos* (the right time) moment was present. In life, you must recognize when there is a destiny helper (a person who gives an opportunity or access you never had before) that is there for you to open a door, gate, or portal and walk through it to the next level. Rahab went from being the queen of brothels and a mogul in Jericho to having a part of Christ's genealogy. She never knew she had a call on her life, but once she began to serve the spies, her divine appointment to her destiny unfolded before her eyes. Many are called, but few are chosen; the separation of the chosen comes from servanthood, which gets you an appointment with God. God is the heart specialist who examines the heart of man.

Serving is part of leadership, but many do not see it in that aspect. Serving means you must hear, direct, lead, follow, obey, instruct, or assist, depending on what and who you are serving. All of those are attributes of leadership. As Christians, you cannot lead people without integrity, righteousness, faithfulness, and honor, and expect to be successful. In God's estate in heaven before time was in existence, Jesus made a statement that was recorded in John 14:2 (KJV). He said: *In my Father's house are many mansions: if it were not so, I would have told you. I am going to prepare a place for you.* In this statement, we see that Jesus emphasizes *"I go to prepare a place for you,"* meaning an environment that will be of assistance to us as sons of God. With this scripture of John 14:2, everything in heaven has a servant mentality because everything in heaven was created to serve the Father. The four living creatures, each having six wings, were full of eyes around and within. And they do not rest day or night, saying: "*Holy, holy, holy, Lord God Almighty, who was and is and is to come!*" Revelation 4:8 (NKJV) And all the angels were standing around the throne and around the elders and the four living creatures; and they fell on their faces before the throne and worshiped God, saying, "*Amen, blessing and glory and wisdom and thanksgiving and honor and power and might, be to our God forever and ever. Amen.*" Revelation 7:12 (ESV)

The number one thing we can observe in those two key verses is elements of worship. There is a demand for worship in heaven before the throne of God. The service all of heaven partakes in *is to worship*. One of the synonyms for worship is "honor"; the way to show honor is by serving. The relevant protocol in the kingdom of God is to worship; that is the seal of approval by God. It signifies that you are in an intimate relationship with him. Your worship is the beginning of honor to God. Worship is the kingdom culture that signifies your love for God. As we worship God on earth, this act demonstrates our love and honor in the same manner that all those in the heavens love and honor God. Earth is the mirror of heaven. Let's look at the book of Genesis where God created all the important things that the earth provides to serve man. In the mind of God, Earth was created to serve humanity and was a place for man to rule. We see in Genesis 1:2b, "*that darkness was on the face of the deep.*" Nobody can serve in darkness. Before God created anything, the earth had to be supernaturally renovated. Light is the representation of life as darkness is to death. After the light was established in the earth as a decree, God then began to set laws in the heavens to accommodate the earth. He created the dry land to attend to man and animal. Water was created for the whales and fish; also land and water were designed for travel in the mind of God. The stars and moon created light in the darkness, which was called night. The sun was instituted to provide light for the day. The sun was bigger, and the clouds were needed to give shade and to store water to eventually shower the land and cool it. Everything the Creator and Founder of the world manufactured has a responsibility and daily task to serve. Are you serving?

The Spiritual Authority on Earth

The Church is the place society goes to when they have issues, looking for guidance and wisdom on how to execute actions in certain situations. It is a place of feeling good, peace, and love. The Greek name for the Church is *ecclesia*, out of the Strong's Concordance. This word means a group of people called out for a special purpose. That purpose was for the church to govern over the spiritual realm on earth as Jesus ruled and reigned in heaven. It designated the new society of which Jesus was the founder, as it was a society knit together by the closest spiritual bonds and altogether independent of space. The service of the Church is to attract the world; Jesus said that in Matthew 5:14 (NLT): "*You are the light of the world—like a city on a hilltop that cannot be hidden.*" When we turn the porch light on, all different types of insects are drawn to it and fly around it. In that same way, the world is drawn to the light of God in the church. Police departments are structured to enforce the law, order, and give protection to an area, city, or nation. They have offices that are high or low in rank, such as captain, chief, lieutenant, sergeant, and so forth. Police are part of a civil force of a national or local government, responsible for the prevention and detection of crime and the maintenance of public order. Their duty is to maintain law and order in society.

Police give society, communities, neighborhoods, and individuals peace of mind if I know that local protection has their best interest in mind. Countries, nations, and islands would be lawless, and there would be many coupes, gangs, and mobs running these places if there wasn't or isn't a strong police force. We have the luxury to call for the authorities when needed. Imagine, instead of paying tax dollars that go to police funding, you must decide which gang or mob you would want protection from. You must pay them money for their abilities. Without police, civilians would be like animals, and society would be like the Darien Gap, which is one of the world's most dangerous jungles—full of drug traffickers, thieves, and poisonous animals. Police are needed. In the Bible, God constitutes law and order in the book of Exodus 20. His Ten Commandments establish moral law in society. Law is run by the authorities. There were no police in biblical times, but the law helped people stay in alignment with morality and crimes such as killing others, and so on. The law policed the people. The law was the policing for the people—don't steal or lie. If you go to jail now, you go for stealing because the law came from the Bible's standpoint. So, Jesus introduced us to his spiritual military department, which is His Church in the book of Matthew 16:18 (KJV): *"And I say also unto thee, that thou art Peter, and upon this rock, I will build my church; and the gates of hell shall not prevail against it."* That was a bold statement, decreeing that the church would have a rank, which was established before policing. The rank levels are apostles, prophets, teachers, pastors, and evangelists.

The police department or a police precinct is the law and order that Jesus made with a statement to His disciples; in other words, the church has the legal right with authority and dominion to rule and to set the law of legislation in the spiritual realm on the earth. These are the services the church brings to a nation, country, island, or continent. The church is like the spiritual police but also is a spiritual authority over sickness and disease for the sick. Ecclesia has been mandated to manifest the kingdom of God with supernatural abilities. What are we mandated to do? To bind and to lose, deliver and heal, command and decree, and to resurrect the dead. There are three departments that give the church (the power and Authority), gifts of the spirit (character), fruits of the spirit, and the seven spirits of God (glory). Jesus Christ our Lord is head of the ecclesia in Luke 4:18 (KJV): *"The Spirit of the Lord is upon me because he hath anointed me to preach the gospel to the poor; he hath sent me to heal the brokenhearted, to preach deliverance to the captives, and recovering of sight to the blind, to set at liberty them that are bruised"*; as Jesus is in heaven; so are we on earth to serve those who are in need.

The Godhead Serves Each Other

The Holy Spirit is God on earth. Jesus is in heaven, and God the Father is in heaven too. Let us focus on the Holy Spirit. He was born on Pentecost, one of the feasts of the Lord. The purpose of the Holy Spirit coming to earth was that all those who surrendered to Jesus would become like Him. Every individual who has said a prayer of salvation to God would be a duplicate of Jesus on earth. In Romans 8:11 (KJV), the scriptures say, *"But if the spirit of Him who raised Jesus from the dead dwells in you, He who raised Christ from the dead will also give life to your mortal bodies through His Spirit who dwells in you."* Every Christian has the same spirit that Jesus had, as the scripture states above. In Romans 8:9 (ESV), the Word says, *"You, however, are controlled not by flesh, but by the Spirit, if the Spirit of God lives in you."* And if anyone does not have the Spirit of Christ, he does not belong to Christ. On all continents at the same time within different time zones, the kingdom of God can be manifested. There are church services that may be happening right now, street meetings, evangelism, conferences, or crusades that are manifesting miracles, signs, wonders, healings, resurrecting the dead. Deliverance, love, and peace are all works of the Holy Spirit.

The Holy Spirit mandates the body of Christ to be like a guide, director, almanac, google, dictionary, navigation, or GPS. Jesus tells us what His work would be once the Holy Spirit comes:

> *I have told you these things while I am still with you. But the Helper (Comforter, Advocate, Intercessor—Counselor, Strengthener, Standby), the Holy Spirit, whom the Father will send in My name [in My place, to represent Me and act on My behalf], He will teach you all things. And He*

will help you remember everything that I have told you.
(John 14:25, NKJV)

Jesus told His disciples the Holy Spirit will come to help and reveal the Son of God to them. The focus of the Holy Spirit is to reveal Jesus to the body of Christ. He is also our Comforter in times of pain, hurt and grief. Whenever we are before the accuser, the Holy Spirit is our Advocate, our true Intercessor to appeal before the courts of heaven. He is the one that counsels us when we need guidance in situations that are bigger than what we can handle. When we are weak and feeble, He is the spirit of strength in us. He is always our standby, never far away from any dilemma or circumstance; the standby is always near. With every supernatural act Jesus demonstrates, a prophetic word is released. The Holy Spirit helps us to understand and gives clarity on the Word of God. We are to imitate Jesus Christ, while the Holy Spirit serves as the revelation of Jesus, which is the Word of God. Jesus's obedience was service, one of respect and honor to the Father. He chose not to repeat the steps of his older brother, the first Adam. First Corinthians 15:45 states, "Thus it is written, *the first man Adam became a living being* the last Adam became a life-giving spirit (Jesus)." In 1 Corinthians 15:22, the Word states, "*For as in Adam all die, so also in Christ shall all be made alive.*"

The primary reason was to be servile as a son and to introduce fatherhood to a world full of orphans; and second, to establish sonship that believers would have an identity that comes from the heavenly Father and not a God of judgment. I only do what I see my father do and say what my father says. That's what Jesus said. In serving, Jesus acknowledged God as Father, and that was the reason for Him going to the cross. He is not working independently but following instructions relegated by the Godhead. Jesus's ministry was to please the Father, and nothing else mattered to him. If the Almighty was satisfied with His actions, the Son was delighted. The Holy Spirit releases revelation to us but Jesus came to teach us the Father's heart and sonship. Lack of a father takes away the revelation of sonship in society. Many believers cannot see God as Father; because many experiences with their natural father are bad, such as rejection, abandonment, or forms of abuse that are mental, verbal, or physical. The character of the Father is servitude to Himself as the head, a good example to His family in mannerisms, vocabulary, leadership, action, work ethic, integrity, and honesty. Children love to be like their dad, as he leads by example. Then later in life when children are serving, they become good, respectful citizens in society, a fruit of their father's action. God is the Father to Jesus, and the Godhead of the Holy Spirit. They are not independent of each other; they're synchronized in covenant, in marriage as one.

In Genesis 1:1, the Bible introduces God first. His Spirit is the creative power of God. As the Father speaks, the Spirit manifests the Word. This is verified in the book of Zechariah 4:6. So he answered and said to me, "*this is the word of the Lord to Zerubbabel, not by might nor by power, but by my spirit; says the lord of hosts.*" God reveals that nothing is created or manifested without His spirit working and He is also pleased with His beloved son as a Father. God is demonstrating a relationship with His offspring, the one He sent to the world to be a living sacrifice of redemption.

Testimony of Jason Brown

Jason Brown was an NFL player and one of the top centers of the league. He was drafted by the Baltimore Ravens for his first three years in the NFL. In 2009, he signed as a free agent center with the St Louis Rams, which got him the biggest signing contract in the NFL at that moment. A $37M contract was awarded to Jason Brown in the fourth year, and he was let go in 2012. During that time, God began the transformation process of Jason's heart. The wealth, fame, and prestige did not give him any satisfaction in his heart. Jason had an older brother named Deuce who had given his life to service by joining the military. His brother passed away in Iraq on September 20, 2003. Deuce's death took a toll on Jason. That was the first turning point in Jason's life. It propelled him to focus and play for his brother, and that is what he did. He became a top player at his position in college and got drafted into the NFL. Process requires a journey, and within the journey you will find the treasures. On his twenty-seventh birthday, he had everything he wanted, and his wife was a dentist; together they were a powerhouse couple. He had nothing to be discouraged about. He designed his whole life to make it on top of the mountain professionally, but finding himself lonely, he gained the whole world, subsequently losing his soul. The second turning point in his life was when he recommitted his relationship with God and put family first.

The NFL was part of the journey to prepare Jason for his purpose and destiny. God birthed servanthood in his heart, changing him from selfishness to selflessness; impacting and becoming influential in a greater way than he could imagine, leaving a legacy for his children to be a part of serving. He walked away from millions of dollars and submitted to God's purpose of service as a farmer. He purchased a 1,000-acre farm that produced a million pounds of sweet potatoes in his hometown in North Carolina. He is more notable as a farmer now than he was as an NFL player. God is amazing. When you recognize your purpose, you will find your true self in this world. Your servanthood brings you into purpose. In servanthood, you become a blessing to a multitude when surrendered to the will of God. Money does not solve problems; people do. It's more of a blessing to give than to receive. Servanthood is a lifestyle of giving that fulfills the heart with satisfaction.

Prayer

Lord Jesus, I humble myself before your throne, in total surrender to you. I repent for not seeing you as a father. I repent for not allowing your process to mature my character. I repent for giving my flesh rights over my spirit. I ask forgiveness for not allowing you to have total Lordship over my life. Wash me in the blood of the lamb right now, Lord Jesus. I renounce every spirit of rebellion, disobedience, and independence in Jesus's name. I break every yoke and curse in my life that causes me to be out of the will of God. I ask for your grace, Father, and to be chosen, by way of service to you, Master Jesus. I will fulfill my purpose through servanthood in Jesus's name. Amen.

CHAPTER 4

Jesus Came to Reveal the Father

*J*esus did His first miracle at the wedding, turning water into wine. He was bringing forth the spiritual marriage of the old and the new; the law and grace, and the blood and water to mirror the natural marriage he attends. The water turned into wine as in Numbers 20:6–11 (KJV):

> "And Moses and Aaron went from the presence of the assembly unto the door of the tabernacle of the congregation, and they fell upon their faces: and the glory of the Lord appeared unto them. And the Lord spake unto Moses, saying, Take the rod, and gather thou the assembly together, thou, and Aaron thy brother, and speak ye unto the rock before their eyes; and it shall give forth his water, and thou shalt bring forth to them water out of the rock: so, thou shalt give the congregation and their beasts drink. And Moses took the rod from before the Lord, as he commanded him. And Moses and Aaron gathered the congregation together before the rock, and he said unto them, hear now, ye rebels; must we fetch you water out of this rock? And Moses lifted up his hand, and with his rod, he smote the rock twice: and the water came out abundantly,

THE HEART OF SERVANTHOOD

*and the congregation drank, and their beasts also. And
the Lord spoke unto Moses and Aaron, because ye believed
me not, to sanctify me in the eyes of the children of Israel,
therefore ye shall not bring this congregation into the land
which I have given them."*

God told Moses to speak to the rock. God was moving from law
to grace, but Moses was stuck in the law, which birthed anger because
the blood was not shed, forgiveness was not granted, and sin was not
tolerated by God the Father. God was transitioning Moses from hitting
(law) into grace by speaking the Word. There was a shift where the Lord
God was introducing Moses back to the beginning as He spoke things
into existence in Genesis. Moses was not ready for change and was not
able to adapt to something new without physical work. Like many of
us, it is hard to accept change but easy to stay in the same cycle. Jesus
went to the Jordan River in Luke 3:21 (NKJV): *"When all the people
were baptized, it came to pass that Jesus also was baptized; and while He
prayed, the heaven was opened."* The Father lives in a heavenly state, so
there was a mandate from this point on that man can live with an open
heaven over their lives. Everything Jesus does refers to God the Father.
Read John 5:19 (NLT) here: So Jesus explained, *"I tell you the truth, the
Son can do nothing by himself. He does only what he sees the Father doing.
Whatever the Father does, the Son will also do."* This is the essence of
a relationship. Outside of a relationship, it is hard to receive instructions or criticism. For you to follow or receive orders, there must be a
relationship. This is the most important demonstration Jesus has given
to us as his followers. The relationship is the key in Christianity; religion does not require a relationship. Religion creates law confusion and
restraints, never fellowship or a feeling of intimacy. Religion teaches to
"do" then to "be" while Christianity is "I am" to "do". Religion has gods
but Christianity has a father.

The meaning of relationship is the way in which two or more con-
cepts, objects, or people are connected or the state of being connected.

It is the state of being connected by blood or marriage. Relationship also means the way in which two or more people or groups regard and behave toward each other. Since this is a world of orphans, Jesus came to restore the hearts of the fathers to the sons and the sons to the fathers. Jesus exhibits what a relationship looks like and what it offers. Miracles, healing, deliverance, casting out devils, and the supernatural are the benefits of a relationship with God. The disciples saw Jesus doing things only the Messiah should be doing, as stated in the different books of the Old Testament. So, they were curious and asked Him to teach them how to pray.

> In this manner, therefore pray: *Our Father in heaven, hallowed be your name. Your kingdom come; your will be done on earth as it is in heaven. Give us today our daily bread. And forgive us our debts as we forgive our debtors. And do not lead us into temptation but deliver us from the evil one. For yours is the kingdom and the power and glory forever. Amen."* Matthew 6:9–13 (NKJV)

There are seven keys to this passage: God is first. The estate is heaven, and it requires a relationship. God is holy. The commonwealth of the king will arrive in the natural as it is in the spirit with day-to-day blessing and forgiveness. We are not guided into temptation. The King's commonwealth is power and glory forever. Jesus was showing the disciples a model of how they should pattern their prayer, starting with the Father. Establishing the Father, Jesus states that God is your source and that all your dependency comes from Him and no one else. Knowing that removes all other questions about who to pray to and who you should expect an answer from.

Many people in Christ grew up without a father in their home. It's difficult for them to identify God as a Father; the lack of identity blocks a true relationship with the Father. Jesus knows that this is an orphan generation, and they are lacking fathers. Jesus shows us that a son always looks to the father with honor, respect, and love. As the Holy Spirit serves Jesus to us by revelation, Jesus serves the Father by being a Son as an example of how to follow and be intimate with the Father. The identity of the Father instilled in Jesus through relationship says *"If you see Me, you have seen the Father. You cannot say that you have not seen the Father, because I and the Father are one"* (John 14:9). (XXXX xx:xx).

The Family Meeting

The Father does nothing without counsel. His priority as Father is family. There's a story in the Bible that speaks about the Tower of Babel, where the people wanted to be like God. They wanted to come up into the heavens. The Father said to the counsel of the Godhead, let us go down (Gen. 11:7) in reference to the Holy Spirit and Jesus, the son of God. Also in Genesis 1:1, the father established himself as the head. In verse 2, the Spirit of God moved over the face of the waters. In verse 3, And God said, let there be light: and there was light; the light is Jesus. God is the Father of light. There is no darkness in him. The Father is always in communication with the Trinity of God. The Father serves Jesus and the Spirit. Just as a business has positions, duties, or responsibilities, God is the CEO, Jesus is the COO, and the Holy Spirit is the executive administrator for all holy activity. God shows us He does nothing without consulting His Son and His Holy Spirit. How much more should we be in communication with God regarding everything in our lives?

The Cross

The cross is not a myth, nor is it a legend. The cross is not just a piece of wood that Jesus was crucified on. *"For the preaching of the cross is foolishness to those who are perishing, but to us who are being saved, it is the power of God"* 1 Corinthian 1:18 (KJV). For the cross has everything that is life, that is, the abundant life in Christ. For every situation or curveball that is thrown at you by the accuser of the brethren, the cross has the solution. Sickness, curses, and poverty are the three hindrances in life that keep all of humanity in bondage and imprisonment. *"Christ hath redeemed us from the curse of the law, being made a curse for us: for it is written, cursed is everyone that hangeth on a tree"* Galatians 3:13 (KJV). He became poor so that we may be rich. He bore all our infirmities, and He became a curse so we may be blessed. Christ defeated the enemy on the cross, and when we carry the cross, we defeat the enemy here and now. The cross is the legacy to humanity. Satan is defeated, destroyed, dethroned, and disarmed. The cross leaves a legacy of victory in every area of our lives. A legacy is passed on to the next generation. Legacy focuses on what will endure. It's about passing on things of lasting value to those who will live on after us. Legacy involves living intentionally and aiming to build into the next generations for their success.

Those who live in darkness are enemies of the cross because they are led by their flesh and not the spirit-man. You befriend the cross as you carry, it and the flesh has no rights or say so in any matter. The cross is the silent assassin to the flesh. Nothing about the cross is natural; it is all supernatural. The cross is the spiritual stimulus system that all debts against us are paid in full and not remembered. Everything the prosecutor tries to charge us with is something the cross exonerates us from. Jesus, as our defender, declares with proof of His blood on the cross and His scars that all debts are paid in full of no pending balance. The case is closed. The beginning of love is forgiveness. The cross displays forgiveness of sins from the past, present, and future. One of the greatest challenges people faces is self-forgiveness. This causes the past to be present. Let's say there's a woman who blames herself for her child dying because she was an alcoholic. Or maybe she had an abortion. She's living with guilt and has no self-forgiveness. Emotionally, she is unstable, and it still haunts her. Once she surrenders her mind and will to the cross, the past becomes present, and she can now become free in her emotions, delivered from guilt. She can now deal with life as a whole person. God restores, and He does it in a big way.

Forgiveness goes before love as praise goes before worship to release the atmosphere from any bondages or heaviness. In that context, forgiveness brings a release to redeem freedom to self. The cell doors open, and the chains and shackles drop off, allowing you to enter another realm of the cross. Worship affirms God and the finished work of Jesus. The cross provides love to them who have a revelation. Love is one aspect of the power of the cross.

As the cross is north-south and east-west, vertical and horizontal, that is how God designed His love to flow. Jesus loved people on all levels of life, the rich and the poor (reflecting the high and low parts of the cross). Love those above you, those at the same level you are on, and those below you. Jesus came to fulfill the law, which says (Mark 12:31) love your neighbor as you love yourself and (Matt 22:37) love the Lord with all your heart, all your soul, and all your mind. Love is the dominating power of the cross, which is a mystery to Satan and his kingdom because there is no love in Satan. God wired all men to desire to be loved, everyone from the gangster to the manly men, children, women, and prostitutes. Love is seen, felt, and heard. The love of God cannot be rejected, neglected, or resisted. The love of God is like a hammer that breaks the hardest of all individuals. One touch of God's love, and that tongue will confess, and knees will bow to Jesus Christ as Lord.

The cross is the authorization and demonstration that Satan was defeated, destroyed, dethroned, and disarmed by Christ going to the cross through Pilate and the religious leaders. When we do not live with the revelation of what Jesus accomplished on the cross, even as believers, we will live a life as if Jesus never was crucified. That is the plan of the enemy's devices—for us to be ignorant.

A Servanthood Heart

Death comes with pain. Pain is the process for conception. Fasting is a deliberate abstinence from physical gratification, usually going without food for a period to achieve a greater spiritual goal. Fasting is intentionally denying the flesh to gain response from the spirit. The pain of fasting is not being able to eat the food you are craving or have a great desire for. Fasting is death to hunger, and it is pain to the flesh. A woman in labor has pain and gives birth to a child. Pain is the process for conception. What does not cost you anything will never have value. Out of the abundance of the heart, we serve. Without a transformed heart, it would be impossible to walk in servanthood. *"Create in me a clean heart, O God, and renew a right spirit within me"* Psalm 51:10 (KJV). *"And I will give you a new heart, and a new spirit I will put within you. And I will remove the heart of stone from your flesh and give you a heart of flesh"* Ezekiel 36:26 (ESV). The heart is the most important organ. All the other organs relate to the heart through the blood. The blood flows out of the heart and is distributed to all organs in the body. A plane has a black box that records everything. In turbulence or after a crash, the black box can assist in finding out what was the cause of the accident. You are what is in your heart.

The truth is in the heart, and it cannot be fake or indifferent. Here is a testimony that explains this. A young lady was killed, and the parents donated her organs. A lady received her heart. As she went to bed, she had a dream of the murder event. God showed her the killer; she saw the murder events unfold in a dream and was able to let the authorities know about it. They caught the murderer. The heart restores all our life events, and the Bible says in Proverbs 4:23 to guard your hearts above all else, there the issues of life flow. The perception of you from others comes from your actions. The fruit of the heart are your words. Service is the ability to help bring satisfaction to the heart. When you do good by serving people—feeding the homeless, helping the elderly, or little kids—your heart feels satisfied.

Time

Everything that lives in time, dies. In our earthly realm where time is measured, everything becomes mature in time. What is the definition of time? It's the indefinite continued progress of existence and events in the past, present, and future. Time is regard to being whole.

A point of time is measured in hours and minutes past midnight or noon. In Ecclesiastes 3:1–8 (KJV), you are probably familiar with God's words on time:

> *There is a time for everything, and a season for every activity under the heavens: a time to be born and a time to die, a time to plant and a time to uproot, a time to kill and a time to heal, a time to tear down and a time to build, a time to weep and a time to laugh, a time to mourn and a time to dance, a time to scatter stones and a time to gather them, a time to embrace and a time to refrain from embracing, a time to search and a time to give up, a time to keep and a time to throw away, a time to tear and a time to mend, a time to be silent and a time to speak, a time to love and a time to hate, a time for war and a time for peace.*

Basically, everything we can experience or go through is in these verses. It really sums all things up. God also calls us to be the reflection of Himself in time. *"And God blessed them, and God said unto them, Be fruitful, and multiply, and replenish the earth, and subdue it: and have dominion over the fish of the sea, and over the fowl of the air, and over every living thing that moveth upon the earth"* Genesis 1:28 (KJV).

Subdue means to overcome, quiet, or bring under control. In Hebrew, it means to bring into bondage, dominate, be underfoot. Synonyms of the word *subdue* are conquer, defeat, overcome, overthrow, reduce, and vanquish. Dominion means sovereignty or control of the territory of a sovereign or government. It means lordship, sovereign, or supreme authority. On earth where time is birthed, God wants us to be as He is in heaven to rule, reign, and have dominion over every species, and over land, water, and air. We are called to be priests and kings on the earth. Time has no authority over the children of God, but we have authority over time. Eternity lives inside us, and that is on the outskirts of time. He that lives in us is greater than he that lives in the world. The world is governed by time, and time dominates the world. The Holy Spirit rules over the world because He is Lord of the supernatural in the earth realm and not bound to time. Time requires evidence of stewardship. To be fruitful is a sign that you're productive, increasing, multiplying, or producing. The Bible said that you will know them by their fruit. Fruit is the evidence of kingdom mentality. Jesus's message to the world was that the kingdom of God is at hand.

Within Time We Serve

In heaven, time does not exist. In heaven, everything is supernatural, and faith is not needed. Only in time, faith is accessed because it is the door into the supernatural. Servanthood is the action it takes to prove ourselves to God. Serving is the method that God uses to mold us, and we become the clay. God, as the potter, shapes us into the image and the likeness of God. The image and likeness of God are the co-inhabitants in servanthood. The dictionary meaning of image is a visual representation of something. We know that God has hands, feet, eyes, a mouth, arms, and heart. He has emotions and all those human parts are in the scripture. Before the football season starts, there is a pre-season. The pre-season determines how many people will be on the team and who will play which position. Your service is like a pre-season into what God has for you. Your faithfulness and obedience determine how long your pre-season will last. When you serve, it is hard for you to abort or backslide from your calling. Endurance and humility are cultivated in serving. They are the builders of character. It is remarkably interesting that Adam and Eve stopped serving and gave their undivided attention to Satan. An intriguing thought is that the Bible never said how long they were distracted. In the glory, there is no time. It was never mentioned, nor can we measure it. Sin (Satan in nature) came and stole Adam's passion to serve God but interrupted time and substituted it for the glory.

Immediately, time began to kill him. God said in Genesis 3:17(KJV): *"cursed is the ground for thy sake; in sorrow shalt thou eat of it all the days of thy life."* The curse was conceived in the beginning through sin, which became time. The curse is the name of the firstborn of sin. Time is the second born. Everything in time has an expiration date, and sin is the mother of time and the curse. After being deported out of the garden, Adam's life became hard, and God's glory was scarce. We see how time became a curse to mankind. God wants us to serve him. Serving allows us to become like him. Our CEO God gave Adam a mandate that kept him in the glory. That is the same method we use to walk in His glory. Two pioneers of their generation that shifted time were Abraham and Noah. *"Now the LORD had said to Abram: "Get out of your country, from your family And from your father's house to a land that I will show you "Genesis* 12:1 (NKJV). God gave Abram instructions on moving, disconnecting, and leaving his family. Abram was separated by God's standards for His holy purpose, calling, and destiny so He could reveal Himself to Abram. The patriarch begins his journey with actions to do and obey, which releases faith. The Father had given him a promise. Interestingly, Abram's name means "exalted father."

Here's the promise in Genesis 12:2–3 (NKJV): *"I will make you a great nation; I will bless you And make your name great, And you shall be a blessing. I will bless those who bless you, And I will curse him who curses you; And in you, all the families of the earth shall be blessed."* God is prophetic. The promises were in chapter 12. When you read the promises, they are right there, and there is significance. There were twelve sons of Jacob whose descendants became the twelve tribes of Israel. There were twelve apostles of Christ Jesus, and there are twelve months of the year.

God sealed His approval of Abraham generations previously to make it a reminder of His promise. It is amazing how God begins the verse in Hebrews 11:1, although it does depend on the version of the Bible you are reading. Now faith is, or faith is now; this chapter aluminates those who lived a life of faith; therefore, Abraham was inducted into the Bible Hall of fame of faith, of which Abraham is the father. God is intentional and prophetic. The number twelve is very powerful. It symbolizes faith. Abram has been declared as the father of faith by the Word. Also, the number *twelve* symbolizes a church in which faith is the foundation of our gathering and demonstrates divine rule.

The Bible says we go from glory to glory and from faith to faith. God took the faith from the Old Testament and reconfigured it into a new dimension of faith in the New Testament. Faith has a new sound, look, act, and demeanor in which He moves. Faith is a person named Jesus, and what Abraham did to please God is what Jesus became to keep Abraham's relevance in the now. God made a covenant with Abram. When God makes a covenant with you, things change around you, in you, and with you. Jacob walked differently after the covenant and encounter with God; he was called to be a nation. Abram's name was changed in Genesis 17. There was an encounter and a covenant God made with Abram. He became the father of many nations. His name became Abraham, which means "father of a multitude." Now Abram's pre-season starts by his serving God with faith, which propels him into his purpose. As he serves in time, he is getting old. Both the promise, which was prophesied by God, time moved on, and the bodies of Sarah and Abraham were maturing. When your focus is on the prophetic word, your heart is not fixed on God. That prophesy will become your God instead of God the Father. I have seen many brothers and sisters in Christ throughout the years place more emphasis on prophecies or prophetic insights than God. Then, because the word spoken to them did not come to pass, they fell by the wayside and began to say that those were false prophecies. When that happens, the person will fall into sin.

What do I mean by falling into sin? When your focus is not on God, your attention will be captured by a distraction. Anything that takes your attention from honoring God is a distraction, which can be a person, place, or thing. A distraction will come because the enemy knows that your focus is not on God, due to your vocabulary and your mannerisms. Not praying, worshiping, seeking God, fasting, and not contending for the prophetic words released over your life mean your focus is not on God. The Bible says in Timothy 6:20 (NIV), *"Timothy, guard what has been entrusted to your care. Turn away the godless chatter and the opposing ideas of what is falsely called knowledge."* This shows that you must do something and not be idle. When you are idle, distraction becomes prevalent. That is the mistake Abraham made by sleeping with his wife's servant, Hagar. He went to God for everything except that situation. He used his own strength because he was pressing upon the promise, instead of the promise giver. All distractions lead you into temptation. The maturity of distraction is sin. Sin is the result lack of intimacy and flirting with temptation. No matter how small a sin/distraction is, the goal is to separate us from God's presence. The word says sin separates us from God.

The promise of Isaac was born. Abraham's season began because he started walking in faith. Man loves the breakthrough, but God loves the process. Abraham's twenty-five years of investment of time pleased God and propelled him into the purpose and calling God had for his life. What you put or place above God becomes a curse.

Prayer

My God, I come in agreement with Your Word and agree to be purified in the blood of Jesus Christ. I humbly submit my heart to you in total surrender, Jesus. I repent for not recognizing you as my father. I repent for not having revealed the cross. I repent for not allowing You to work in my heart. I ask for grace to know You as my heavenly Father. I activate the cross to manifest in my life from this day on. I draw healing, deliverance, miracles, power, provision, and love from the cross of Christ. I am activated to be supernatural with grace on earth to do miracles, signs, wonders and to resurrect the dead in the end times.

Amen.

CHAPTER 5

The Love of Servanthood

God is love, but love is not God. There are two men in the Bible who gave God their entire hearts and served the Father without limitations, King David and Apostle John, disciple of Christ. Jesus displayed love and service to the majesty (God) above all other men. David served Saul who competed with him and came to hate David. God called David to be a king, and David was also placed to serve the king. Serving the man or woman of God is the metamorphosis to carry the legacy in the future. In servitude, there is a reciprocation of the anointing or mantle that is activated upon your life. In 1 Samuel 16:18, it is remarkably interesting to see how David was described to be a king, but until he served the man that was in the position, the Lord hid him. There are six main points about David.

First, David was the son of Jesse from Bethlehem. He was a skillful musician who came to serve the presence of God. David was a carrier of the presence of God due to his worship and romancing the Spirit of God and God the Father. The Word says that in the presence of God is the fullness of joy. Saul needed peace at the time because he was being tormented by spirits. The second description of David in this passage called him brave and nonpassive. A king should have a courageous heart that is fearless and very efficient. Third, David was a warrior with a "never back down" attitude. Another word for warrior is a service person to protect a territory. The fourth description shows David to be very insightful to see, feel, and perceive. He was handsome and very likable.

Fifth, God Almighty was with King David and not Saul. Sixth, the submission to King Saul gave David access to what living like a king. He was getting first-hand experience of being the ruler over a nation. This was the exchange of guards from young to old, or from the former glory to the latter glory. The son of Jesse from Bethlehem served. What is so dynamic about serving is that it shows a heart of obedience. On the other hand, Saul never served anyone and became a king. You cannot lead the people when you have not served the people in that capacity. This is the reason Saul rebelled, failed, disobeyed, and disappointed God to the point He Himself repented 1 Samuel 15:11. Therefore a pupil or student needs to have a mentor. While running from Saul in the wilderness, David was totally in love with God the father and served with a pure heart.

John Served with Love

Apostle John was one of the twelve that Father God gave to Jesus. Out of the twelve disciples of Jesus, John had a different relationship with Jesus. His full attention geared to Jesus's sayings and parables; he was a reliable disciple to Jesus. He loved Jesus, and in the book of John, love is written fifty-seven times, three times more than any of the other gospels. In the Bible, love is mentioned 310 times. There are three moments that define the love of John in the Bible. John was part of Jesus's inner circle, which is a sign of trust. Not everyone could be spiritually intimate with Jesus, but John was a part of that relationship with Christ himself. John was always one of the three called to be with Jesus in prayer away from the other nine disciples. The inner circle of Jesus included Peter and James, the brother of John as well. On the Mount of the Transfiguration story in Matthew in 17:2, Jesus took them to a high mountain. The mountain represents revelation and insight, and He was transfigured before them. His face did shine as the sun, and His raiment was as white as light. Jesus exposed them to his glory realm. In Matthew 17:3, Moses and Elijah came and spoke with Jesus. Jesus manifested in his natural state of his glory. Moses represents the Torah (the Law), Elijah (the Prophets) and Jesus transfigured as the (King of glory). After that, the voice of the Father spoke out the cloud of glory and we can read it here from Matthew 17:5 (KJV): "*While he yet spake, behold a bright cloud overshadowed them; and behold a voice out of the cloud, which said, This is my beloved son, in whom I am well pleased; hear ye him.*"

John was included in the witnessing of that glory encounter with the Father of heaven and earth. It was a very intimate moment and not by coincidence; it was purposely done. First, John's love was demonstrated at the cross. He was the only disciple who was at the cross. John witnessed the unbearable pain, torture, and death of Jesus, along with Mary his mother. Any disciple or association with Jesus risked being crucified with Christ if they had been seen. John's love for Jesus was greater than his fear of dying. Love is not fearful, nor is love intimidated. God did not give us a spirit of fear, but of power, love, and sound mind (1 Timothy 1:7). John was the last disciple to see Jesus in the flesh as a man on the earth. Second, at the Last Supper, Jesus explained to the disciples that someone would betray Him. John placed his head on Jesus's chest and asked who it was. Jesus said, "the one I give the sop to." John's revelation of Jesus was so affectionate that none of the other disciples could fathom now what John was doing.

Love is irresistible and cannot be rejected. Love brings unity. Love is contagious. When we abide in love, we neutralize Satan, and he can't use us. Third, the moment John was on the island of Patmos was special. It was on the Lord's Day. John was worshiping and heard the voice and encountered the Lord Jesus Himself in the glory realm. It was a call to come up higher; to see what eyes have not seen nor what ears have not heard. The book of Revelation I call it the book of glory, the atmosphere of heaven is the glory of God. The revelation was given to Apostle John with benevolence on the Lord's Day. The Bible says these three remain: faith, hope, and love; but the greatest of them all is love (1 Cor 13:13). The book of Revelation was served from the position of intimacy.

King David: A Man of Service

David served the majesty with worship, which is the presence of God. Word came back to King David that God blessed Obed-Edom, which created a desire to worship and dance before the Lord. Obed-Edom was not part of the Jewish people of their town. His land was a Gentile land, uncircumcised and without a covenant to the God of Abraham, Isaac, and Jacob. God does not just bless people to be blessed. He did not acknowledge him for who he is. There was something Obed-Edom was doing to provoke the sovereignty of God to breathe upon everything that was within his property. God's goodness is always in reciprocation to worship. He delights in worship that is intentionally given and set apart for Him alone. There was a time when David rejected the presence of God. This is like many people once they do not like something God does, or when they think God did something that was not right. Sometimes it's simply that those things they don't like do not go with their theology of who God is. They can leave, quit, and go elsewhere. We can never understand God Almighty in His vast ways. David went to serve God in worship and honor to retrieve the Ark of the Covenant that held God's presence. He decided to go worship the presence of God with dancing, leaping, praising, and worshiping the Lord prophetically with his entire being. As he danced, all his garments came off, and he was not ashamed. Worship is a spiritual service of sacrifice that ministers to God.

His public worship towards his heavenly Father offended his wife, Michal, who was Saul's daughter; this is written in 2 Samuel 6:16b. She despised him in her heart. When David returned home to bless his own family, Michal, the daughter of Saul, came out to meet him. *"She said in disgust, 'How distinguished the king of Israel looked today, shamelessly*

exposing himself to the servant girls as any vulgar person might do!'" 2nd
Samuel 6:20 (NLT). This is an illustration that the leaves of a tree do not
fall far from the tree. Michal had the DNA of her father's jealousy and
envy toward her husband for giving God honor. In the same way King
Saul, Michal's father, wanted to kill David because the presence of God
was with David and not him. He was in competition, jealous, envious,
and willing to kill David (1 Samuel 18:7–9). Michal was not mentioned
ever again in the Bible. As we read in the above verse from Michal,
spontaneous worship publicly offends people, even those closest to you.
Worship is an addiction for God.

Everything about God is supernatural, and He demands to be worshiped. The throne room of God is unshakeable and as the angel cried
out, "Holy, holy, holy, the Lord God Almighty" in Isaiah 6:4 (NIV), their
voices shook the doorpost in heaven. Therefore, we know that worship can shake the heavens and get heaven's attention. A king is honored when he's giving a service of worship, which is a spiritual sacrifice.
Even when David was herding sheep in the desert, his worship was an
offering that attracted God to the house of Jesse of Bethlehem. His worship captivated the animals' attention too. The presence associated with
the worship brought peace and was protection from the lion, bear, and
wild animals. Later, David was even called to minister to King Saul as
he played the harp with wonderful melodies. He released the peace of
God's kingdom with deliverance that shifts the atmosphere and airways
with the presence of God.

King David made a vow to Jonathan, and years later, he served
Jonathan's handicapped son Mephibosheth and invited him to dine
at the king's table. He removed Mephibosheth out of Lo-debar, which
means "stress, depression, low-esteem, and out of a place of shame."
Jonathan saved David's life before he became king, and he served David
despite how his father felt toward David. May I propose this question to
you: are you willing to serve someone who will bless your next generation? Are you willing to make a sacrifice of serving? Serving requires
sacrifice, and obedience is greater than sacrifice. When you serve in any

capacity, sacrifice and obedience come with that territory. The times David disobeyed the Lord were times he suffered. Those were the times he did not go to war with the military, the times he committed adultery with Bathsheba, when he had her husband killed, and when he rejected carrying the presence of God to the city of David.

Testimony of a Husband

Suree is an African American woman like most people in church who come, sit down, listen, and leave without congregating or fellowshipping with the brethren. She was a good friend of mine, and I considered her my sister in Christ. However, her mindset was that she did not need a mentor, nor did she need to serve in the house of God. We attended the same ministry and Bible school. She said that her husband would be from her own race. Years later, she had a mentor and delighted in serving in the usher ministry. Suree surrendered her life to serve the people in the temple of God. I remembered the joy and glow over her face as she spoke about serving. She was a changed woman. Her heart had been transformed to serve God's people, but most important she was being process by God in her servitude. She had met her husband Mario while serving.

Even though she believed her husband would be African American also, God had another plan for her. He is Spanish and now she is part owner of an insurance company they run together. Most believers in the church desire to get married or find their better half. The revelation for marriage in the Bible is serving. Every single individual in the Bible who met their spouse was through in servanthood, starting with Adam, Abraham, Jacob, Boaz, Rahab the harlot, and Esther, to name a few. There is no law that you must serve to get married. But when you do serve, God blesses you with your heart desire. The heart is what God examines, that your actions are not motivated for selfish reasons or pride. One of the fruits servanthood produces by God is a spouse.

Prayer

Heavenly Father,

I present my heart before You and I repent for my sin of being fearful and afraid, intimidated, jealous, envious, timid, doubtful, and feeling shame. I ask forgiveness for being indifferent, passive, non-confrontative, and religious. Lord Jesus, cleanse me with the blood of the lamb. I humble myself before You, Lord, and surrender all of me to You, Jesus. Right now, I make a covenant with you to walk in faith. Let my heart be filled with faith so that I may bring pleasure to You. I declare divine grace that I am motivated by Your supernatural love in my servanthood and for Your will to be done in my life. Amen.

CHAPTER 6

Being a Servant in Christ

(Serving the Spirit of Mammon)

*M*any are called but there are few servants in the church of Jesus Christ. Think of all the churches around the world—every Sunday hundreds, thousands, and millions of people go in and come out of church doors. How many of those women, men, young adults, or children are serving to help carry the burden of that ministry? Serving should be a mentality just as living with money is a necessity. Many Christians serve mammon and not Jesus. What is mammon? Mammon in Greek is *mammonas* in Aramaic; it is defined as riches, money, possessions, and property. Mammonas is a semitic term for "the treasure a person trusts in" *"No man can serve two masters: for either he will hate the one and love the other; or else he will hold to the one and despise the other. Ye cannot serve God and mammon"* Matthew 6:24 (KJV). Jesus is saying money is a god that the church or His people will serve if the servanthood of Christ does not enter the heart of the body of Christ. Many today use the tithes and offerings as talismans to get from God but not to serve him; they use it only for what they can get.

Many people go to church, but they are not *in* Christ. Being in Him requires you to serve. Everyone who is "*in*" Christ has the heart or desire to serve. When we are not serving, we have the characteristics of Satan himself. He did not want to be a servant of God in the worship ministry anymore; the iniquity in his heart desired to replace God on the throne. Satan got kicked out of heaven by declining to serve. When you are not serving people, you easily become offended. Many Christians serve with their lips, but serving God is the action of love. Roaming around with an orphan spirit is the characteristic of Satan himself. Isn't it amazing how natural it is in a family to get the kids to do chores like taking out the garbage, cleaning the yard, washing the dishes after dinner, and making sure their rooms are clean? They are all serving to help keep the house tidy. It behooves parents to set chores or responsibilities for the week; they help children stay in the moral state and consciousness of serving. The children realize they are making a difference in that home without getting a stimulus check. As they get older, that training will help keep them "*in*" Christ because this life is not a sprint but a marathon in the lifestyle of servanthood.

Martha "OUT" and Mary "IN"

Two of the most important functions in the body of Christ are servanthood and worship. The sisters Mary and Martha represent this to the fullest. Any time Jesus tells a story, He's using it to teach or make you realize the great significance of it. He wants you to read it repeatedly and find the mysteries in it. I've heard sermons that bash Martha and exalt Mary; however, the sisters were doing kingdom functions. There are three questions everyone that serves should ask the Lord about themselves: (1) Why am I serving? (2) Am I motivated to be seen? And (3) Do I have an agenda or intention for serving? It is important that we focus on the task to serve with excellence and to give our total attention to Jesus. We want to keep the eyes of our hearts on Him. In Luke 10:38, we read that Martha's eyes and heart were fixated on Jesus, which is awesome and wonderful; but in Luke 10:40, something happened, and she was disconnected from the presence of Jesus while He was in her home.

Being overwhelmed, she was distracted with working. Martha was doing everything from the natural realm, and no part of her being related to Jesus in the spirit. Was her heart in the right place while serving? Both sisters were in the house and in the presence of Jesus, yet the only one who gave Him her undivided attention was Mary. I do not think Martha was wrong, but I believe her heart was not in the right place. There are many pastors and leaders in the body of Christ that are guilty of the same thing as Martha. They are so busy, occupied, troubled with many things within the ministry, and their hearts are far from God's presence. They are doing everything from a natural state of being. Ministry is not a natural calling or job. It is a spiritual office, and if you are not continually in the spirit with your heart aligned with Christ, it's not the right place to be. Wherever there is a lack of Jesus in ministry, divine knowledge is nonexistent, and the advantage is gained by the enemy. Ignorance is the pathway to perish and to death spiritually or even naturally.

> Now while they were on their way, it occurred that Jesus entered a certain village, and a woman named Martha received and welcomed Him into her house. And she had a sister named Mary, who sat at the Lord's feet and was listening to His teaching. But Martha [overly occupied and too busy] was distracted with much serving; and she came up to Him and said, Lord, is it nothing to you that my sister has left me to serve alone? Tell her then to help me [to lend a hand and do her part along with me]! But the Lord replied to her by saying, Martha, Martha, you are anxious and troubled about many things; There is need of only one or but a few things. Mary has chosen

the good portion [that which is to her advantage], which
shall not be taken away from her. Luke 10:38–42 (AMP)

Jesus exposed the other side of serving when there is no intimacy. Jesus in the text above revealed the heart of Martha, she was distracted with much serving. I have seen firsthand that many serve God but use that as a substitute for their relationship with God. When serving without intimacy with God your no longer focus on the things above, you become a complainer and talk about what everyone is not doing. Religion requires work and not relationship. Humility and humbleness come out of servanthood. Luke 10:39 states that Mary sat at the Lord's feet, which is the lowest place to go in serving the Lord Jesus. Her heart was in ecstasy with the Lord and His teachings. All of Mary's being paid attention to Jesus's presence. In John 11:32–33, Mary experienced the death of her brother Lazarus. Jesus appeared on the scene four days later. When she came to the location where Jesus was, she fell at his feet, saying to Him, Lord, if thou hadst been here, my brother would not have died. When Jesus saw her weeping with the Jews who came with her, He was deeply moved in spirit, and was troubled. Mary of Bethany is *"in"* Jesus and worships with a grieving heart, missing her brother Lazarus.

As she worshiped and bowed to the Lord in her loss, Jesus felt her pain and grief, which moved Him in His humanity. In every passage that mentions Mary of Bethany, she had such a reverence and revelation that Jesus was the Christ. She demonstrates reverence by her posture to Jesus the son of God every time he was in Bethany. Mary of Bethany was *"in"* Jesus constantly, surrendering before him in such great humility. Here are three verses Mary of Bethany shows her love and honor toward Jesus. The first was giving the alabaster box and washing His feet (Luke 7:36–50). The second was sitting at His feet (Luke 10:38–42), and the third was recorded in John 11:28–33, kneeling at His feet in public. It is amazing that the Holy Spirit chose to talk about Mary of Bethany several times, which says a lot about her heart in pursuit of Jesus.

The Kingdom Is *Within*

No one can become a new creature if they are not "*in*" Christ. Everything outside of Jesus is old, dead, perverted, and spoiled. The scripture states in 2 Corinthians 5:17 (KJV), "*Therefore if any man is in Christ, he is a new creature: old things are passed away; behold, all things become new.*" When we are "in" Christ, there is spiritual change, transitioning into something and becoming a metamorphosis in—our mind, thoughts, imagination, hearts, spirit, soul, attitude, action, perspective, and vocabulary. All of those are parts of your being, and when they are not renewed, your being is covered in darkness. The Word of God is truth, and God does not lie. The Word says all things become new; God is saying once you decide to receive My Son Jesus, newness and change is part of your lifestyle while walking with the Messiah. Protection only comes when we are in Christ. Protection is guaranteed to sons and daughters. And on that day, when evening came, He said to them, 'Let us go over to the other side,' and having sent away the crowd, they took Him with [them], as He was, in the ship. But other ships also were with Him. And there comes a violent gust of wind, and the waves beat into the ship so that it is already filled. And He was in the stern sleeping on the cushion.

> *And He was in the hinder part of the ship, asleep on a pillow: . . . and awake him, and say unto him, Master, carest thou not that we perish? And He arose, and rebuked the wind, and said unto the sea, Peace, be still. And the wind ceased, and there was a great calm. And He said to them, Why are ye so fearful? How is it that ye have no faith? And they feared exceedingly, and said one to another, What manner of man is this, that even the wind and the sea obey Him? Mark 4:38–41 (KJV)*

Jesus was asleep at the bottom of the ship, resting in the Father. The storm was attacking the ship and the disciples' lives were in danger. There is a lesson during the story that Jesus wanted us to have a revelation about. The things we preach about the disciples in that spiritual confrontation may have been faithless. Jesus and his disciples were sailing to the island of the Gadarenes. Before arriving arose a great storm. Jesus was at the bottom of the boat resting, and the disciples were on the top deck. They saw the boat rocking from side to side, the waves towering over the boat, and the water filling the boat. Their faith evaporated, and they were paralyzed with fear. The fear also gripped their hearts along with doubt and worry. They were afraid for their lives. Jesus was in the ship right there with his disciples. Yet their lack of faith made them feel distant. All Christians face that reality daily—it's the same lack of faith the disciples experienced on the boat. One of the enemy's strategies is to attack your ship (relationship) with Lord Jesus in it. Psalm 37:7 (AMP) states, *"Be still before the Lord; wait patiently for him and entrust yourself to Him."*

There is a promise in the verse above—being still before the Lord. There's nothing about being anxious in the verse. Waiting is the key. Being patient shows that you trust God with your circumstance. The best place to be when there's a hurricane, situation, circumstance, or hardship is one where you have the assurance you are fully covered. As Jesus says, in my Father's house there are many mansions, and out of kinship there are many different ships, figuratively speaking. Our relationship with Jesus, the Holy Spirit, and God the Father requires us to be in many of these different ships with the King of kings.

Below is a list of some of the "ships" you will find in life:

- Fellowship—friendly associations, especially with people who share one's interests
- Friendship—a relationship between friends

- Sonship—the relationship between a father and a son
- Relationship—the state of being connected by blood or marriage
- Discipleship—the process of guiding someone to become like Christ
- Mentorship—the influence, guidance, or direction given by a mentor
- Partnership—a relationship resembling a legal arrangement, usu-ally involving close cooperation between parties with specified and joint rights and responsibilities
- Leadership—the action of leading a group of people or an organization
- Ownership—the act, state, or right of possessing something
- Worship—the feeling or expression of reverence and adoration for a deity

Despise Not Small Beginnings

You are disqualified from your destiny once you despise small beginnings. Despising small beginnings constrains and restricts God from displaying what He created you for. Serving takes you from the unknown and the hidden to become known and visible to all eyes. We know the story that David defeated Goliath and became king. The Lord was testing his heart and his obedience in the small responsibilities handed to him. They may have seemed insignificant in his eyes but had great implications for the nation of Israel. The food that David brought to his brothers represented strength, fulfillment, energy, nour-ishment, love, care, and livelihood. In 1 Samuel 17:8–58, Goliath of the Philistines was threatening King Saul's military. Goliath's idea was that a man from Saul's army would fight him, and whoever lost would become the servant of the winner. He was instigating a battle. Israel's entire army feared Goliath, and if no one challenged him within forty days, Israel would become a slave of the Philistines.

David's father Jesse sent food for the military through David, who had a divine appointment to exterminate Goliath for Israel. When he arrived, David saw the army and King Saul were defeated, demoralized, discouraged, conquered, and paralyzed with fear. These feelings were in the atmosphere. Goliath smelled it and saw their body language. God's giant killer served the Palestine giant his death certificate, and the victory was served to Israel by grace. David's act of service revived the spirit of the army and nation once the giant was destroyed. In the spirit, Prophet Elijah heard a promise from God before it manifested in the natural. Elijah went to initiate that which he had heard from the living God of Israel. In the spirit, he heard rain of abundance—a *mega* sound— but when the prophet began to pray, what the servant saw manifested was not equivalent to what was heard. The cloud was as big as a human fist, the scripture says in 1 Kings 18:44. Most Christians today would start to complain to the Lord, "I heard it was going to be an abundance, but there are only tiny clouds."

The rain that Elijah heard was the finished work of the Lord's craftsmanship. The Lord God declares the end from the beginning, but in the natural world, we all must begin with a small beginner's faith. The Word says in Isaiah 46:10, Declaring the end from the beginning, God in His sovereignty showed him His extravagant nature and the completeness of God. Elijah had to work his faith until the cloud became what he heard. Faith comes by hearing; without action, it is dead. His action was to tell Ahab to go because the rain was coming. As he began to run, the clouds and wind started to form, and darkness took over the landscape. Never despise small beginnings in things because everything that God creates is small and becomes enormous, hefty, colossal, mega, and massive. In the smallness is where God's tests come into play, like a car check-engine light coming on as a warning. God's test is a heart check to see whether you are purpose driven or whether motives have gripped your heart. In the smallness is the place where the character is built. You are known by God before people recognize who you are. *"He that is faithful in that which is least is faithful also in much: and he that is unjust in the least is unjust also in much"* Luke 16:10 (KJV). Let God be the truth and every man a liar. He honors His Word because His Word is what framed and formed the earth. Do not despise small beginnings.

Jesus Fed the Thousands Twice

Jesus ministered, healed, delivered, preached, or taught the people the gospel of the kingdom. This was a service like what every man or woman in the fivefold ministry does. If you are in ministry, it is a call to serve the people of God and the sinners. It is not for the man or woman of God to strive to become popular, famous, or a celebrity. By default, you become famous because of the demonstration of the kingdom of God manifesting through you. People desire deliverance, healing, breakthrough, or blessings. Striving to be popular was not the design for ministry. Now Jesus was going from city to city and the crowd was following and as he looked at them, He saw compassion and healed their sicknesses Matthew 14:14. He saw they had a problem, and he had the answer. When there is good service given, you have peace. Jesus served them through healing, which released peace into their bodies. He realized they were unable to walk more than a day's journey to get back home. They were worn out, tired, and had not eaten anything at all. *"But Jesus said unto them, they need not depart; give ye them food to eat"* Matthew 14:16 (KJV).

He had five loaves of bread and two fishes. This was all that was available to feed them. Five plus two equals seven, the number that represents completion or fullness. He served them the Word of God and served them food to nourish their bodies. They fed 5,000 men, not including wives and children. Jesus pulled off this service without a catering company or servers to pass out the food. It was the manifestation of the miraculous. Everything about that event was supernatural. It is impossible to administer food to nearly 15,000 people with just five loaves and two fish. They experienced firsthand the power of multiplication. All that was done with small beginnings. All this happened while healing the blind, the maimed, the dumb, and the lame. In the next verse, Matthew 15:32, we read about His compassion for their physical body needs: As the people glorified the God of Israel and Jesus had compassion upon the multitude because they continue with me now three days and have nothing to eat, and I will not send them away fasting, lest they faint in the way.

Do you see the needs of people around you? The needs of the people permit supernatural service to their problem. As Jesus saw a need in the multitudes, He desired for us to see the needs of the people, to meet them, and to serve the people in the supernatural power and love of the Father. *"And he took the seven loaves and small fishes; and gave thanks and broke them and gave the disciples and the disciples gave to the multitude* Matthew 15:36 (KJV). The breaking of bread is a sign of humility, which is an attribute that comes from serving. Humility is a trait that comes from servanthood. The making of a man is in his serving, and servitude is love in action. The demonstration of the kingdom of God occurred right there with 4,000 men, not including the wives and children. Jesus is the King, and the kingdom has everything within it—miracles, needs fulfilled, and more. Kingdom service brings satisfaction and excellence to the recipients. With kingdom service, we can experience the above and beyond of God's kingdom.

The Attitude of Service

Servitude has an attitude and a mindset, especially when we are serving on behalf of the Lord God Almighty. The fear of the Lord is our guide to servanthood in the name of the Lord Jesus. In Psalm 2:11, scripture states: *"Serve the Lord with reverent fear and rejoice with trembling."* You are not allowed to include lying, corruption, wickedness, and unrighteousness among your mannerisms while you are serving. Eli's sons were scoundrels, and their sin was very great in the Lord's sight. They were treating the Lord's offering with contempt. They demonstrated no fear of the Lord as priests of Israel. As a servant of God, the fear of the Lord should be the standard for everything you do. The fear of God is one of the seven spirits of God in Isaiah 11:2 (KJV): *"The spirit of the Lord shall rest upon Him, the spirit of wisdom and understanding, the spirit of counsel and might, the spirit of knowledge and the fear of the Lord."* The last on the list is the spirit of the fear of the Lord, and the Bible says the last shall be first and the first shall be last. The fear of the Lord should be the beginning of all things. Proverbs 9:10 (NIV) states, *"The fear of the Lord is the beginning of wisdom; and the knowledge of the holy God is understanding."* Without the fear of the Lord, wisdom has not even been conceived. The fear of the Lord is the prerequisite of wisdom.

Serving Without the Fear of God

In a Samuel 2:12, God called Eli's sons "sons of Belial." Beli means "without" and al "to be valued of." In Hebrew, the name Belial is characterized as the wicked or worthless. It is also another name for Satan or for antichrist. God spoke to Eli about disciplining his sons or removing them from their duty as priests of Israel, but Eli did not do either. He allowed his sons' bad behaviors to continue in the house of the Lord. He did not have the fear of the lord. When you have the fear of the Lord, you will depart from evil, and your understanding is to walk in the light of righteousness. Psalm 25:14 (NKJV) says, *"The secret of the LORD [is] with them that fear him; and he will show them his covenant."* The Lord will release secrets to those who fear him. Eli stopped hearing from the Lord. Samuel had to relay a message of what the Lord was going to do to the house of Eli. His eyes were dim (blind), and he was overweight.

The function of a priest was not Eli's focus because he stopped fasting and continued to indulge in eating the contaminated offerings his sons were releasing. The offerings were considered "strange fire," offerings that were not accepted and considered defiled by God. A priest is called to pray and fast. *"The light of the body is the eye: if therefore thine eye be single, thy whole body shall be full of light. But if thine eyes be evil, thy whole body shall be full of darkness"* Matthew 6:22–23 (KJV). If therefore the light that is in you is darkness, how great is that darkness! In 1 Samuel 4:15, we learn more about the latter years of Eli's life. Eli was ninety-eight years old; and his eyes were so dim that he could not see. He watched his offspring do evil before the Lord, and he had no restriction toward them regarding their behaviors. It caused his life and legacy to be cut off. This story of Eli and his kids is a lesson ministers of the gospel should take seriously and never allow to happen in their calling from God.

Supernatural Maids

Most kings, queens, presidents, prime ministers, and the rich have bodyguards and servants who care for them in their homes and when they are away. They also have cooks, maids, security, and property care-takers around the property. In the same way that country leaders have security and help, so do the children of God within the earth. God has given us the ministry of angels, and there are different types that help with different kinds of situation. *"Therefore, angels are only ser-vants—spirits sent to care for people who will inherit"* Hebrews 1:14 NLT. They are assigned to serve us in many different capacities in life and have their own servanthood to the Lord as well. Let's look at some sto-ries from the Bible and stories of how people interacted with angels, speaking of their service. In the verses of 1 Kings 19:6–7 KJV *"And he looked, and behold, there was a cake baked on the coals and a vase of water at his head. And he did eat and drink and laid him down again. And the angel of the Lord came again the second time, and touched him, and said, Arise and eat; because the journey is too great for thee."*

We see that Elijah was in the desert and tired, worn out, depressed, discouraged, and fearful because of the words he had heard from Jezebel's servant. In 1 Kings 19:2 (NIV), scripture states, *"May the gods deal with me, be it ever so severely if by this time tomorrow. I do not make your life like that of one of them."* She was referring to the prophets that Elijah killed, that the same thing will happen to him. That caused Elijah to run away from the witch, fearful that he would die. He never rejected the word of the witch. Instead, he believed it in his heart as he journeyed a day into the wilderness, fearful of death. An angel came and made him hot bread and water. The angel woke him up twice. After the second time, he was awake. The meal from the angel rejuvenated, strengthened, empowered, and built him up for the travel of forty days and nights to Mount Horeb. Angels are "supernatural butlers" to serve the heirs of salvation; they were also great cooks who brought food from heaven that strengthened Elijah. As the Lord provided for Israel in the wilderness with fresh manna, water was also provided to Israel by God for his people.

In the same way, we have policemen who are essential workers to serve to protect society; in like manner, angels are doing the same for the children of God. How are they protecting us against the kingdom of darkness? In Psalm 91:11–12 (AMP), scripture states, *"For He will command His angels regarding you, to protect and defend and guard you in all your ways of obedience and service. It says, they will lift you up in their hands so that you do not [even] strike your foot against a stone."* Angels are spiritual bodyguards with supernatural ability, strength, and might. They serve protection from evil and wicked assignments, plans, strategies, and tactics so the enemy will not prosper against the servants and children of God. Even in the book of Daniel, he was thrown in the lion's den and the lion's mouth was shut supernaturally by angels who were there for the righteous. Psalm 34:19 (KJV) states, *The eyes of the Lord are upon the righteous, and his ears are open unto their cry";* that is, a promise of help and covering. The last story for protection is from 2 Kings 6:12. Elisha had heard every plan the king of Aram had discussed in his house, and he was upset with Elisha because Elisha had warned the king of Israel to not go to a certain area where there was a trap. He had sent a strong team of soldiers to capture Elisha.

The servant of Elisha woke up and looked out of the cave, saw the soldiers, and was afraid. So, the prophet said to his servant in 2 Kings 6:16 (NIV), "Don't be afraid," the prophet answered. "Those who are with us are more than those who are with them." Then he prayed that the eyes of his servant would be opened to see the army of angels. The environment was full of horses and chariots of fire surrounding them, far out numbering only fifty soldiers sent to arrest Elisha. We always have protection by angels sent by God to watch over the words he spoke and impregnated in us that it may be performed. Angels are governed by the Word of God, and the ministers aid us with supernatural strength by the commands based on God's Word. They harken to the Word of God, and they excel in strength as said in the book of Psalms in 103:20 (KJV) "Bless the Lord, ye his angels, that excel in strength, that do his commandments, hearkening unto the voice of his word." As the Bible says in our Father's prayer for the kingdom of God to come and be done on earth as it is in heaven, when angels come into your atmosphere, eternity invades that place. When Jesus was fasting in the desert for forty days, the devil confronted him when he was weak.

Angels came and ministered to him. They strengthened him, not once but twice. Even while in the Garden of Gethsemane, He sweated blood and was weakened physically, but the angel of the Lord came and ministered to Jesus as he was going to the cross for the sins of all humanity past, present, and future. Sarai was angry with Abram and mistreated Hagar. While in the wilderness, pregnant with Ishmael, the angel of the Lord met Hagar. In the wilderness the angel encouraged Hagar to return and to submit to her master. He provided fresh water for her and instructed her to return to Sarai. Even though the promise was not with Hagar, the angel came because she was carrying the seed of Abram. The sin of Sodom and Gomorrah occurred before the Lord released judgment to the city. Two angels were sent to destroy all who were not in right standing with God. Angels came to judge the city as Abraham stood in the gap, interceding for righteous people. God saved Lot's family; angels enforced God's will upon the earth. The only family that was allowed to leave was Lot's. The men of the city were so perverted and sinful that they wanted to sleep with the angels. Lot and his family were told to leave immediately with the instructions, and not to turn around or look backward because they would die. The fire was going to rain upon the city. All this was due to the sin and iniquity of those who lived there.

While the Israelites were in Egypt, God released the angel of death upon Pharaoh's house. Judgment was initiated by God over Egypt, but God protected Israel with blood on their doorposts. All firstborns, humans, and animals, of Egypt died. Not one of the Israelites died. God sent judgment but grace was given to the children of God. In the New Testament after Jesus was crucified, and the disciples were being persecuted, King Herod in Acts 12:23 took the honor and glory from God. An angel came and struck him down. He was eaten by worms and died. Do not steal the glory of God and think there will be no consequences and judgment. Messages are sent from the throne of God to earth via angels. What God thinks, desires, created, and wants for you is delivered by angelic beings. The Word of God is the creative power of God himself; in the book of Genesis, He demonstrates and displays how great His Word is. The Word says, "for the letter kills, but the Spirit gives life" in 2 Corinthians 3:6. What makes the Bible come alive is the inspiration from the breath of God. The breath of God is the semen that gives birth to the Word of God. "Ruach" in Hebrew means wind, spirit, and breath. In Psalm 104:4 (NASB), the Word says, "*He makes the winds His messengers, flames of fire His servants,*" so the winds of God are His messengers.

The winds are angels that carry His Word and make sure His Word is accomplished. In Isaiah 55:11 (KJV), scripture states, "*So shall my word be that goes forth out of my mouth. It shall not return unto me void, but it shall accomplish that which I please, and it shall prosper in the thing whereto I sent it.*" The Lord creates what He says and if it depends upon a person, angels will help and assist for that which was declared to be manifest through the person that obeys the Word. The Word was in the beginning, and the Word is settled in the heavens. In heaven, the Word is blessed, prosperous, peaceful, alive, quick, powerful, creative, authoritative, glorious, and magnificent. The Word is like water. Wherever there's water, life abounds. And he shall be like a tree planted by the rivers of water, that bringeth forth his fruit in his season; his leaf also shall not wither, and whatsoever he doeth shall prosper. Ps. 1:3. You have fruit, and you prosper when aligned and plant yourself within the Word of God. *"For the word of God is quick, and powerful, and sharper than any two-edged sword, piercing even to the dividing asunder of soul and spirit, and of the joints and marrow, and is a discerner of the thoughts and intents of the heart"* Hebrews 4:12 (KJV).

The only thing in the realm of time that can examine or discern the heart of man is the Word of God, which also separates the soul from the spirit of man. When we use the Word and when we look and sound like God, the Word is a birth canal. We see God give a message sent with angels to be delivered to earth. The angel came and spoke to a young virgin girl, Mary. In Luke 1:28 (NKJV) it says, *And having come in, the angel said to her, "Rejoice highly favored one, the Lord is with you: blessed are you among women."* The message to Mary was that she was honored, favored, and chosen among many other women. That means that the Lord stopped at many other women's houses and saw that they never met the requirements of the Lord's demands to birth the Messiah. Mary was honored, blessed with favor, chosen by God, and favored with God. She was a vessel for the purpose and will of God. Mary was in service to God. See! You are to become a mother and have a son. You are to give Him the name Jesus. He will be great. He will be called the Son of the Highest.

The Lord God will give Him the place where his early father David sat. He will be King over the family of Jacob forever and His kingdom will have no end in reference to Luke 1:31–33. This was a messenger angel from heaven named Gabriel. It was hard for Mary to accept she was chosen from the throne of heaven. She questioned what was told and how it would happen because she was a virgin and because of who her fiancé was. God had a plan for Joseph and arranged a dream for him. The angels released the message to him to marry Mary. Also, six months prior, Zachariah had had his own encounter with Gabriel, and he did not want to cooperate, so without Zachariah's assistance, God got his way. For the whole nine months, Zachariah was muted, his tongue was tied, and he could not talk because of his doubt and reasoned why it could not happen; all of that was unbelief. Zachariah was a priest, a man of God; the Bible says he was a righteous man. We see you can be a man of God, preaching the Word without believing what you are preaching, especially when an encounter manifests itself for God's will to prosper through you. Angels can release messages in full form, visions, dreams, or in prayer. There are many services angels provide to us as the heirs of salvation. They are constantly around us, looking and waiting to provide services mandated from the throne of God on our behalf. The Lord of Hosts is effortlessly working to serve and assist the body of Christ.

He Came to Serve and Not Be Served

Whenever it's election time, most politicians have commercials on TV. They say at the end of the message, "I approve this message." Serving endorses and approves of the kingdom of God; the supernatural purpose is to serve as God would. In the book of Genesis, we are called gods to act like God. In the book of Ephesians 5:1 (NLT), scripture says, "*Imitate God therefore in everything you do because you are His dear children.*" The purpose of the education of heaven is to serve; God came to serve humanity. "*Even as the Son of man came not to be ministered unto, but to minister, and to give his life as a ransom for many*" Matthew 20:28 (KJV). So, Jesus came to serve man, the world, and the Church. The whole Bible is about serving and becoming a servant; that is the greatest revelation in the kingdom. Jesus's statement, "I came to serve and not be served" is a death sentence to His will by authorizing the potter to shape and mold the clay. God tests you in serving. Out of serving He can trust you. Maturity comes through serving, which is the activity of preparation. Serving is a dedication to giving your life away. When you keep your life, you lose it.

Affirmation and approval come from serving. Serving is a key; serving creates a walk with God. Serving cultivates a friendship with God. Serving generates a heart after God. Serving births sons and daughters. If you have seen me, you've seen the Father; serving draws you face to face with God. Jesus is the master servant, the excellence and epitome of what serving produces. A woman who does not like to serve will never become a good helpmate. In the book of Genesis, a woman is called to serve, meaning to help or assist her husband with the responsibility he has been given by God. There is a saying that a woman makes a house, but a wife makes a home. In a family, the woman is the one that establishes organization. Women were made from the characteristics of God with the grace to multitask with ease. I have a friend whose wife makes great money as a pharmacist. They decided that he would stay home with the kids and not work. At first it sounded like a good idea, but he was in for a rude awakening. The duties were waking up early, making breakfast, cleaning up the house, doing laundry, washing dishes, and preparing dinner. There is always something to do, and you are never off the clock. After a couple of months, he realized how important the woman's responsibility was as she helped him serve their family. The respect and honor that he had for his wife was greater than before, causing their relationship to become more synchronized as one. He had a revelation of how life would be without a wife and mother as his helper. After a couple months, he decided to return to work because the work at home was greater as a stay-at-home dad than someone with a job. When a woman does not serve her husband as a helpmate, the relationship will become dysfunctional, and vice versa with the man.

Prayer

Holy God of Israel, I repent for the spirit of mammon. I repent for despising small beginnings. I repent for not being aligned to the will of God. Cleanse me in the blood of Jesus. Wash me white as snow. I activate the power of the cross of Jesus Christ. I thank you, Father, for the grace so the kingdom of God will work and move within me. I thank you, Father, for the attitude of servanthood. I thank you, Lord God, for the fear of the Lord and angels that are supernatural beings to assist the heirs of salvation. The kingdom of heaven is backing me up in Jesus's name. Amen.

CHAPTER 7

The Services of the Armor of God

Supernatural Apparel

*E*verything God designed, created, or birthed has a responsibility to serve. All supernatural assistance is to aid and help us as sons and daughters to be victorious in this realm. The Word of God is supernatural, and it gives us a battle garment to stand and engage in spiritual warfare against an enemy that does not have a physical body. It is our supernatural covering of protection that also equips us for combat to contend and to release a spiritual onslaught of ammunition against demonic forces in times of trouble. The armor of God is not seen in nature. You must believe by faith you have it on. It never comes off. In John 20:29 (NKJV), Jesus talks about not seeing and believing: *Jesus said to him, "Thomas because you have seen Me, you have believed. Blessed are those who have not seen and yet have believed."* Thomas had Jesus before him and still did not believe His words. Jesus is telling us to believe and trust. Thomas did not believe or trust the Old Testament, which was already written about the coming Messiah. Everything Jesus was teaching and talking about shows that Thomas was not listening to hear.

Now today you and I have the Bible, by reading the Word of God that speaks of His son. Faith comes by hearing the Word of God, believe by faith and trusting comes by faith, which Thomas at that moment did not have. The fruit of that on our part is being blessed; that is your reward. Nothing about our salvation is natural; it opens the door to a supernatural lifestyle in the power of God and requires supernatural armor to persevere and to withstand the wiles of the enemy. The armor of God is the endorsement of your relationship with God in your life because it is a walk by faith and not by sight. Look at Ephesians 6:10 (KJV) for a minute: *"Finally, my brethren, be strong in the Lord and in the power of His might."* In the last part of the verse, look at the two words "Be strong," which is a command of action. The apostle gave us an instruction on how not to be weak, and how to be a force. We are only strong if we are *in* the Lord and immersed in the power of His might. The key is being *in Him*, which requires a current relationship with God. This is a position that must be established. Paul gave us a revelation of how he was able to have dominion over the enemy. Being in Jesus guarantees victory. Here's part of the proof in Colossians 3:1 (ESV) *"If then you have been raised with Christ, seek the things that are above, where Christ is; seated at the right hand of God."*

The emphasis is on "in the Lord" because the right hand of God signifies power, might, strength, authority, and provision. Those are the blessings and benefits of being "in the Lord." As He is in heaven, so are we on earth. Outside of Jesus, we are no confrontive, fearful, defeated, ignorant, and act as a footstool for the kingdom of darkness to reign upon. You probably already know the Ephesians 6:11 (KJV) by heart: *"Put on the whole armor of God, that you may be able to stand against the wiles of the devil."* The key word in this verse is *stand*, which is in the New Testament 153 times according to Strong's Concordance. One definition of stand is to take an upright position. Another definition defines it "to remain firm or steadfast." When you stand, you are being aggressive, fearless, and ready for any engagement of warfare. You have the attitude and posture of a warrior who can conquer. Between both verses of Ephesians 6:10 and 11, the apostle gives us three keys that should be a lifestyle of the supernatural: (1) being strong; (2) in the Lord; and (3) power, which provides the ability to stand.

Now that you have the general overview for the spiritual armor, it's time to look at the individual components.

1. Shoes of Peace

Naturally many people believe the most important part of the body is the heart or brain. Without any movement and activity, blood clots occur. The feet are a very intricate part of the body. A man's feet are made to take authority, position, stand, movement, and walking, never being stagnant. In Ephesians 6:15 (KJV), we see: "*And your feet shod with the preparation of the gospel of peace, which the gospel is the good news of Jesus Christ.*" Preaching the gospel brings peace to us personally and peace between God and man. How beautiful are the feet of those that preach the gospel. The Bible says that the steps of a good man are ordered by the Lord (Psalm 37:23). If you are led by God, He is the God of peace, and because of your obedience, your life will have an abundance of peace. Peace is the lamp to our feet and light to our path (Psalm 119:105). When you're not able to see ahead of you, you're walking in darkness; therefore, you will lack confidence and not walk in faith. Revelation is the light of the word that releases peace because you know that is the will of God from the peace within.

If you are full of anxiety and worry going into a battle or war, you have already lost the fight. Even in war, there must be peace to create strategies and plans. Strategies and plans cannot be created or fully executed if you are frustrated or stressed. You need peace to follow through with the commands or instructions. As we investigate the armor of God, look at how the Father has equipped us to have peace as protection and as an offense on a spiritual level. The Lord has approved of us and encourages us to clothe ourselves with the Word of God. He is faithful, and His Word declares, (Jeremiah 23:39) "I will never leave you nor forsake you," so keep it on!

The armor of God serves every part of our body. When we walk, there are shoes that command peace to be under our feet. Whenever we arrive anywhere as sons and daughters of God, if there's chaos, destruction, or tension, we can enforce peace to override any atmosphere. Out of all the parts of the armor of God, peace is probably the one that people speak of the least as a weapon. Peace can be seen, felt, and heard. When a woman has financial confidence, love, and protection in her marriage from her husband, she knows that there's stability, security, and harmony. Peace becomes the atmosphere that she carries.

That peace in the atmosphere is the supernatural peace that keeps a marriage or relationship together in Christ. Peace is a supernatural glue that sustains a marriage or relationship, and it commands attraction to an atmosphere. Stress screams divorce, chaos, confusion; quite frankly no one wants to be around heaviness, darkness, noisiness, and evilness. In contrast, peace speaks and declares unity. What is the definition of peace? Peace is the absence of chaos and the absence of hostility. Peace regulates the mind of people. Peace can be in the atmosphere of places and things. Merriam Webster's dictionary says peace is a state of tranquility or quiet.

Peace is the force of heaven. In this spiritual war we fight, peace is an atomic bomb against the kingdom of darkness. There is no peace in darkness, wickedness, or evilness. Peace is the atmosphere of heaven. Peace is one of the signs God uses to introduce Himself, and its purpose is the advancement of His kingdom. Whenever Jesus walked around, He had two phrases He would usually say. One of them is "the kingdom of heaven is at hand." This one established the domain of His kingdom, and a kingdom must have a king. A kingdom procession does not come into a place unless the king is in attendance. The atmosphere cannot be hostile wherever a king is residing. Peace is also a refuge for our mind and heart. In Philippians 4:7, scripture says: And the peace of God, which transcends all understanding, will guard your hearts and your minds in Christ Jesus. God's peace surpasses your natural thinking, mindset, and understanding, which mankind cannot comprehend. Peace is also a refuge for your mind and heart especially whenever your mind panics or thinks the worst and your heart beats what seems like a hundred times a minute. How do you obtain peace?

Worship and prayer are the driving force to cultivate peace. There is no restaurant, mall, bank, or store where peace can be bought, auctioned off, or placed on layaway. Peace is available to everyone, but not everyone desires to sacrifice to apprehend peace. It's possible that the rich do not have peace. When addicted to drugs and alcohol, there's no peace. And, when trusting in money, not God, it doesn't take long to find out that money alone gets you nowhere. *It is easier for a camel to go through the eye of a needle than for a rich man to enter into the kingdom of God* Mark 10:25 (KJV). People with financial hardship do not have peace. It is only when you can set your financial hardships aside and realize that God is in control and will lead you out of them, that you can regain peace. Criminals involved in financial scams, gamblers, and those that do ungodly things for money to try to make it economically do not have peace. Peace avoids the poor and the rich, but after surrendering to Jesus, they can experience the peace of God. It is a feeling that satisfies the soul; experiencing this peace only once will cause a craving for it again. The peace of God is something we are supposed to want to taste and experience repeatedly. What is the kingdom of God? We get part of the answer in Romans 14:17 (KJV): "*For the kingdom of God is not meat and drink, but righteousness, and peace, and joy in the Holy Ghost.*"

How can you live in righteousness, peace, and joy outside of the Holy Spirit? The requirements for all three are in the Holy Spirit. Peace is a fruit. It's one of the nine fruits of the spirit. The Lord said in Matthew 7:16 that you may know them by their fruit. The type of fruit you carry confirms the kingdom that you're in a relationship with. The Father of peace, the Lord of peace, the prince of peace, the King of peace, and the Spirit of peace is where you want to be. I have a friend who works in the medical field and deals with patients who need chemotherapy. Every day she communicates with a family member or the patient directly. She hears them vent. Some are angry, especially if they are denied insurance coverage and need to be seen for treatment. They want to explain the severity of the pain they are experiencing and how it is affecting their lives. One of the diseases she spoke of was amyotrophic lateral sclerosis (ALS), a progressive nervous system disease that affects nerve cells in the brain and spinal cord, causing loss of muscle control. She couldn't help but cry when the patient speaks of their inability to be independent as a spouse or parent and the level of pain they endure. Peace is prosperity in our health on a mental, emotional, and physical level. Third John 1:2 (NKJV) states, *"Beloved, I wish above all things that you may prosper and be in health, as your soul prospers."*

Who is the prince of peace? Jesus is the peace mankind is seeking, and He is called the prince of peace. Peace is the very force of heaven. God uses peace as a bomb. We see this here in Mark 4:39 (KJV): *And he arose, and rebuked the wind, and said unto the sea, peace, be still. And the wind ceased, and there was a great calm.* Imagine what it would have been like to be there. The waves are roaring, and the winds are blowing. It's a chaotic picture for the disciples, and yet Jesus is asleep. He wakes up and speaks to the wind, which is the atmosphere and to the seas. Do you know how much force and power it takes to override a storm to come into tranquility? He had to override the storm and manifest peace in the environment. The sign of God's power is His peace. His words were enough to stop the massive storm and bring calmness to the situation. There's a force to peace, and this example shows how He was able to stop the chaos in the natural realm. Peace be still.

2. Belt of Truth

Truth is the quality or being true, conforming to fact or reality, exactness, steadfastness, and faithfulness. It's the practice of speaking what is truth, freedom from falsehood, and in righteousness to assert something as true or to declare. In John 1:9–10 (AMP), the scripture states, "*There it was the true Light [the genuine, perfect, steadfast Light] which, coming into the world, enlightens everyone. He (Christ) was in the world, and though the world was made through Him, the world did not recognize Him.*" John starts out his book talking about the beginning of time in the first verse. John 1:1 (AMP) says, "*In the beginning [before all-time] was the Word (Christ), and the Word was with God, and the Word was God Himself*" The truth keeps the whole armor together. The belt of truth is for your waist and keeps the armor balanced. In society, we see young men in urban communities not using a belt to hold up their pants. Not wearing a belt is a sign of disorder and rebellion. It is interesting that where there is no truth, corruption rules and reigns. When God releases truth, there is no condemnation, only compassion and love. Where there is truth, there is no shame, guilt, or condemnation. On the other hand, when the devil brings a lie, it comes with shame, guilt, and condemnation. It keeps you in bondage. This is one way to recognize what is from God and what is from the enemy. Are there any lies in your life that are keeping you in bondage? *"And you shall know the truth, and the truth will set you free"* John 8:32 (NKJV).

Truth is the gavel the righteous judge uses to crush Satan's plans in the courts of heaven. Truth keeps you in agreement, alignment, and in covenant with God. Truth is not what the devil has. The devil has nothing in him that can speak the truth. He is full and embedded with lies. Kryptonite is to Superman as truth is to the devil. Truth is the light for darkness. Jesus is full of truth and no lie is in Him. Truth is straight. There is no crookedness, and it is without apologies or apologizing. Truth allows the authority and grace of God's power to be manifested. The belt of truth serves us to keep us in right standing with God Almighty. Truth is a protection, but a lie is an open door for the enemy to attack, take territory, and manifest his kingdom in and through you. You may ask what an open door is? It is anything that is ungodly and will give authority to the enemy. If you steal something, you create an open door, so it's better to tell the truth. If you lie, that is an open door, so tell the truth. If you sin, that is an open door, so tell the truth of what you did and repent. Repentance restores you back to God and removes any accusation against you. The key to closing any open doors that the enemy has access to is repenting before God. Isaiah 43:25 (NKJV) states this: *"I am He who blots out your transgressions for my own sake, and I will not remember your sins."* So, the verse above is saying once you repent through the blood of Jesus, He removes any sin against you, and He remembers it no more. What an awesome God and Father we serve.

3. Breastplate of Righteousness

The armor of God covers all parts of the body. The breastplate covers the torso where all the internal organs lie. The heart is one of the most important organs that the breastplate protects. Each day, the heart beats about 100,000 times. The heart is the engine of the body and pumps about 2,000 gallons of blood through the body per day. Heart is cited 826 times in the *Strong's Exhaustive Concordance of the Bible*. Your words identify the state of your heart. The fruit of your words comes from the heart. Luke 6:48b (NKJV) confirms this: *"For out of the abundance of the heart the mouth speaks."* The Lord wants us to live in righteousness. Righteousness is a lifestyle or a way of living, a state of being in right standing with God in everything we do. That does not mean we are perfect. The only perfect man who ever walked the earth was Jesus, and there will not be another. Romans 3:23 (ESV) reports this to us: *"For all have sinned and fall short of the glory."* Every man that walks this earth except Jesus has sinned. Not one of us on earth is perfect; we will sin. What is the definition of sin? It is an immoral act against God or divine law. Sins are considered actions, any thought, word, or act considered immoral, selfish, shameful, or harmful. Wikipedia defines it as a lie, sexual thought, stealing, exaggeration, or curse word. His grace and repentance through the blood restores us to righteousness. Lamentation 3:22 (NKJV) is one of my favorite verses: *"Through the*

Lord's mercies we are not consumed, because His compassion fails not. They are new every morning; great is Your faithfulness."

Our consciousness, thoughts, sight, hearing, and imagination are a few things that God wants righteousness to rule over. God never does anything without a purpose. There is always value and significance when given instruction to do something. The breastplate of righteousness protects the heart. *"Keep your heart with all diligence, for out of it springs the issues of life"* Proverbs 4:23 (NKJV). A child watching his or her mother being abused physically and/or verbally, or a child who has been molested or raped will be affected just as much as an adult. Some of the issues that manifest from these traumas include becoming anti-social, alcoholic, a drug addict, suspicious, lack of trust, or having a hard time to build relationships. Our life experiences arise from the heart, and there the good and bad is stored. The heart is our most vital organ. God created our skeletal system in such a way as to protect the heart. Yet, we are taught in (Jeremiah 17:9 KJV)" *The heart is deceitful above all things, and desperately wicked: who can know it?"* In the scripture above, the Word of God shows us that the heart is deceitful and wicked. Many women and men who are incarcerated have done some horrific crimes like murder, even cannibalism, having sex with a corpse, rape, theft, and molestation, to name a few. They are in prison because of the action that stemmed from the fruit of their heart.

God knows all things. Although we cannot know the heart of another person, we can discern parts of the heart by watching for the fruits. The Bible says that you will know them by their fruit. The fruits of the heart are the words out of one's mouth, for out of the abundance of the heart, the mouth speaks; whatever is in our heart is what comes out of the mouth. In Matthew 5:8, we are told it is possible to be pure in heart. Blessed is the pure in heart, for they shall see the Lord. The ability to see the Lord God Almighty in physical form is dependent on having a pure heart. One of the synonyms for righteous is pure. The psalmist says in Psalm 51:10 (NKJV): *"Create in me a clean heart, O God; and renew a right spirit within me."* The heart and spirit must be on the same page; the psalmist is crying out for a heart that is purified. He wants his spirit to be aligned with his heart. David was a man after God's heart. Here is the connection to the armor: the breastplate serves and protects us from offense, bitterness, unforgiveness, and being offended. It protects us against heart attacks, which is a diabolical attack from darkness.

And it offers us protection against mistreatment from people and relationships. I remember as a teenager that my dad was very angry, short tempered, and verbally abusive to my siblings, mother, and me. Hate is a strong word to use but honestly, that is what I felt in my heart toward him at the time; freedom for me was him not being in the house. As I got older, I had unforgiveness in my heart toward him even though I never knew it at the time. Once I surrendered my life to Jesus and was saved, I recognized I had to forgive to build a relationship with my dad. Today, my dad and I have great communication, respect, honor, and love for each other. The righteousness of God came into my heart, allowing me to be in right standing with God. Now my heart has compassion, is tender and sensitive, and there is a conviction with the fear of the Lord. "*Therefore, be imitators of God as dear children*" Ephesians 5:1(NKJV). To imitate God, we must be children of righteousness to follow the God of righteousness. We cannot imitate God with a heart that is not like God. *The steps of a righteous man are ordered by the Lord and the prayer of the righteous avails much.* God intentionally guides your path to His will. Obedience puts you in right standing with God. When we are righteous before God, our prayers are limitless to what we can accomplish with God on earth.

4. Helmet of Salvation

Warfare Territory

Territory is taken, or territory is lost between your ears. The helmet of salvation prevents territory from being taken or lost. What is salvation? The Greek word *soteria* is defined as deliverance, welfare, prosperity, and safety. The greatest weapon against Satan's kingdom is having the mind of Christ. If your mind is like that of Christ, there would be less influence of the kingdom of darkness. It would enable you to act like God. *"Let this mind be in you, which was also in Christ Jesus"* Philippians 2:5 (KJV). Why do we need the helmet of salvation? What does it produce in our life? Our head houses the brain that controls our body. It is the tower that communicates what to do to the rest of our body. Our brain is the chief executive of operations to direct our limbs. The most important thing to know about the mind is that it's a territory. The mind is a battleground where there is warfare in every human being. The war is between two kingdoms in operation: the kingdom of God and the kingdom of Satan. Only one will establish authority in that space. The mind is the liability or weakness of all followers of Christ because sin was birthed there and brought forth the fall of man. Iniquity came into Lucifer. *"You were perfect in all ways from the day you were created, till iniquity was found in you"* Ezekiel 28:15 (NKJV).

God is holy; therefore, we know there was no sin in heaven. As the war in heaven took place in the book of Revelation, Satan and his angels were cast out immediately like lightning. There is no tolerance for sin in heaven where God resides. In Luke 10:18 (NLT), we read, *"Yes,"* he told them, *"I saw Satan fall from heaven like lightning."* Jesus was telling the people Satan was evicted out of heaven so fast it was like lightning. The mind is the place sin is conceived to influence man. Since the mind is the most powerful part of the body, it needs covering. The armor of God includes the helmet to ward off the targeted attacks of the devil. His goal is straightforward: to steal, kill, destroy, and derail our lives. The helmet of salvation helps us rightfully sustain working out our salvation through the mind, through the consciousness, the subconscious, and imagination. What do I mean by working out our salvation? First, let us define salvation. Salvation is the state of being saved or protected. Salvation generally refers to the deliverance of the soul from sin and its consequences. Working out your salvation is basically pursuing spiritual maturity. The requirement of sustaining your salvation is work, to spend time with God in prayer, the Word, and worship. There must be sacrifice and God as a priority in your life to work your salvation. Spiritual maturity comes from knowing God. Let's say you have an open vision of Jesus who says, I love you. This vision will prompt you to learn all about Him by reading His Word. You learn his character, mannerisms, regulations, conduct, and His heart in His Word. By reading the Word of God, it transforms your mind, consciousness, subconsciousness, and imagination, so you won't be like the world.

You want to please Him after reading His Word. *"And do not be conformed to this world, but be transformed by the renewing of your mind, that you may prove what is that good and acceptable and perfect will of God"* Romans 12:2 (NKJV). We must constantly live a lifestyle of renewing our mind with the Word, allowing us to prove what is the good, acceptable, and perfect will of God. When we read the Word of God, we have the mind of Christ because His Word is His mind in writing. The Word governs over the soul, which consists of the mind, will, and emotions. The Word distributes faith to those areas. The Word is alive and powerful; it is a sharp double-edged sword that cuts, removes, and washes things that oppose the will of God in us. Imagine a bucket of water with a lid on top. The lid has not been removed for two weeks. What would the water in the bucket look like? What would it smell like? Most likely the water will change colors and there would be an odor. Dirty dishes require dishwashing liquid to wash them clean and sanitize them. Dirty clothes require detergent, so our clothes are clean and fresh scented. In like manner, the Word of God is a cleansing agent that keeps the mind pure, fresh, alert, quickened, and sharp. In the book of Genesis, God saw and then spoke. It is in the imagination of God where the blueprint of creation was founded. Then He spoke into existence of what He had seen. Therefore, having a clean and pure mind helps us have a healthy lifestyle in faith as sons and daughters of God.

Mental Illnesses and Disease

You may be wondering what the relationship of mental disease is to the helmet of salvation. The relationship depends on how you approach your Christian life. When you are casual about your Christian life, that's when unholy, ungodly, and unrighteous thoughts will cultivate. They may materialize as perversion, fear, double-mindedness, unbelief, and even to the extreme of mental illness, such as dementia, bipolar, and schizophrenia. Amnesia could be another manifestation; this is another situation where someone has literally lost his or her mind. Those are the fruits of darkness, which come to occupy because the mind was not covered. The occupation of the devil is to steal, kill, and destroy the lives of humanity. One way to explain this is that a tree does not grow over-night; it takes time. It is the same thing with the thoughts in the mind. It takes a while for these unrighteous thoughts to bring a harvest. In Genesis, Satan is called the old serpent. Satan is wise and he is cunning, has guile, and is crafty enough to trap you into his plans. He has been around long before you and me. In Galatians 5:9 scripture states, "*A little leaven leavens the whole lump.*" He knows that sin begins as a seed, and it grows over time. A married man may be addicted to porn, but it started when he was a little kid looking at Playboy magazines. Those imaginations in the mind no longer satisfy the flesh; now it desires live moments of pornography. Even though he has a woman next to him, his flesh craves and desires a sexual endeavor with another woman.

Sin brings us harm. In Romans 6:23 (KJV), the Word says, "*For the wages of sin is death.*" Wage is a payment, usually money for labor or services. It's usually made according to a contract and on an hourly, daily, or piecework basis. A wage is a payment for services to a worker, and that remuneration is on an hourly, daily, or weekly basis. In Romans 6:23 (NKJV), scripture states: "*The compensation for sinning is death*"; there must be activity or work for sin to occur. Death could be spiritual and/or natural; before anything happens in the natural realm, it takes place in the spirit first. Death is the fruit of sin and temptation is the mother of sin. Our faith is contaminated by the demands of temptation, which are signals to the mind and a door to the flesh through our eyes, ears, thoughts, and imaginations. *"Clarity and purity be sober-minded; be watchful. Your adversary the devil prowls around like a roaring lion, seeking someone to devour"* 1 Peter 5:8 (KJV). With this verse, God is revealing the attitude of our enemy and exposing his traits so we can identify the enemy in the spirit or natural realm in situations that come forth. At the beginning of the verse, God gives the revelation of how to unmask the enemy before He even tries to attack us.

To answer the second part of the question, the helmet of salvation produces soberness and the act of being watchful. You cannot watch if you are not sober. If you are not sober, you are influenced by intoxication. Being sober is being alert, aware, level-headed, and the opposite of drunkenness. God says beware, you have an adversary. An adversary means either a person, a group, or force that opposes or attacks, or an opponent, an enemy, the adversary, the devil, or Satan. When one comes to oppose and resist you while you are sober-minded and watchful, you will see straight through the lies of the deceiver. If you are not sober, deception will become a developer that builds on the real estate, which is your mind. The lion is the king of the animal kingdom, while Jesus is the lion of Judah and the lamb.

Deceit

The revelation is that Satan is a chihuahua that sounds like a lion. The enemy always tries to be like God, but he is not. God wants our mind to be sober. If it is not sober, the enemy takes captive the executive command of our free will to influence us to be disobedient. In the same way, he deceived Adam and Eve to obtain that master key to have us live in rebellion. The devil was evicted out of heaven by God Almighty and stripped of his heavenly citizenship. Any living being on earth fulfills the requirement to have a body. As humans, we have a spirit and a body; that makes us legal on earth. Once we die, we are gone from the earth.

We decompose. The devil is a spirit without a body, which makes him and his minions illegal on earth. Yet he wants to be here and is here but not in human form. To manifest, he needs a human body. Satan was a spirit in the Garden of Eden and had to inhabit a body—that of a serpent—to be on earth legally. He can inhabit people as well. It's why the Bible says we don't fight against flesh and blood. We are fighting against spirits. Spirits become legal inside a human body, and that is when they can do their destruction—to steal, kill, and destroy.

Jesus had to come on earth via a human body because He was a spirit, and He couldn't violate God's law. The only legal individuals on the earth were Adam and Eve. Genesis 2:7 (NKJV) states this: "*And the Lord God formed man from the dust of the ground and breathed into his nostrils the breath of life; and man became a living being.*" We are the living beings on earth that God breathed life into our nostrils; that gives us legal rights on earth. How can an illegal alien have access to the White House of the United States, the Department of the Treasury, or to the United States Department of Defense? That would be a security breach. Before that individual is given any legal rights to be in this country, the immigration officials will and must identify your documents that give a legal representation of residency in this country to work in such a high-security environment. The thief does not come except to steal, and to kill, and to destroy. But Jesus stated, "*I have come that they may have life and that they may have it more abundantly*" John 10:10b (NKJV).

Submission to God

Putting on the helmet of salvation in the spirit is a declaration of submitting to God and His will and resisting the devil. "*Therefore, submit to God. Resist the devil and he will flee from you*" James 4:7 (KJV). Not even Jesus was able to totally stop the enemy from attacking his mind, and He could not resist Satan unless He was submitted to God first. When someone mentions the kitchen, automatically you know that is where food is created, made, and processed. The mind is the place where temptation fertilizes the imagination with sinful pictures and activities. In 1 Corinthians 10:13 (NKJV), the Bible says: *"No temptation has overtaken you except such as is common to man, but God is faithful, who will not allow you to be tempted, beyond what you are able, but with temptation God will also, make of the escape, that you may be able to bear it."*

> The spirit of the world is around us. *"In which you once walked according to the course of this world, according to the prince of the power of the air, the spirit who now works in the sons of disobedience"* Ephesians 2:2 (NKJV).

The world is governed by the prince of the power of the air. This spirit works in the children of disobedience. We need to be covered with the armor of God, which is putting on the Word of God, our spiritual clothing, ensuring that the enemy does not have an advantage over us. Finally, God wants His bride to be sober and watchful. He wants us not to be blinded or overcome by darkness. He wants our mind to be in the light, so our imagination can flow and partner with the Holy Spirit to be like gods on earth as Jesus is in heaven. He wants His kingdom to manifest in and through us for His will to be done on earth as it is in heaven. The priority for anyone that says they love God is to keep their mind aligned to Jesus. *"In whom the god of this world hath blinded the mind of them which believe not, lest the light of the glorious gospel of Christ who is the image of God, should shine unto them"* 2 Corinthians 4:4 (NKJV).

5. Sword of the Spirit

The Word of God is supernatural, which is the voice of God in writing. That is what God said over thousands of years ago, but even today everything we face in our lives has an answer. The answers are found in the Word of God. Nothing about the Word of God is natural. The Bible is not a normal book. Hebrews 4:12 (KJV) tells us about the Word of God: *"For the Word of God is quick, and powerful, and sharper than any two-edged sword, piercing even to the dividing asunder of soul and spirit, and of the joints and marrow, and is a discerner of the thoughts and intents of the heart."* The Word defines this verse and what the sword of the spirit is. Quick, powerful, sharp two-edged sword, piercing of soul and spirit, joint and marrow, it discerns the thoughts and intentions of the heart. The Bible, which is the Word of God, is supernatural. My uncle was illiterate. When he was a teenager, he dropped out of school to help care for his younger siblings. This hindered his education and prevented him from becoming a success. Some missionaries came to the school and gave the kids a New Testament Bible. They told them not to keep the book on the dresser or on the shelf. He was insecure and intimidated by individuals who spoke well and graduated from high school or college.

In his heart, he was terrified, fearful, and timid when around individuals with those accomplishments. He left the Bahamas in 1980 and came to Miami, Florida, a day before Thanksgiving as a teenager. He was eighteen years old with a second- or third grade reading level. Not only was he illiterate, but he had been sick with diarrhea for years. The only book he had was his Bible, and he began to read with the little knowledge of what he had learned in elementary school. The Bible was his guide to literacy; after several months of reading, his confidence was restored. He learned words he could not pronounce or write. The Word of God bestowed in him the gifts of understanding, knowledge, and wisdom. After months of reading the Bible, he realized that he was also delivered from his stomach illness. He had received healing and became strong in vocabulary and writing. Also, six years later, he bought his first house after coming to America with only $800 in his pocket. There are many stories of people that did not know how to read or write but learned how by reading the Bible. The Word of God is a weapon to serve the body of Christ, and an unbeliever who is willing to believe. Its purpose is to subjugate and subdue the works of the devil, confronting darkness and evil spirits that wage war against us. *And I say unto you Peter, upon this rock I will build my church and the gates of hell shall not prevail against it* Matthew 16:18 (NKJV).

The Word is a rock. It's for all Christians to build a strong foundation, so God can establish his kingdom on earth. The revelation is that the church is founded on the rock, which is Christ Jesus, Yeshua Hamashiach. Anything the church or the body of Christ builds upon will be tested by fire. If it's not in the Word, it will not stand and will burn up. There are a few ways the Word of God can be digested, but we will focus on just two of them. The first one is the written Word that in Greek is called *logos*. The second is the voice of God. Logos is God's voice in written form. It is a sword in the spirit; God is a spirit, and anything that comes from Him is spirit. *From His mouth comes a sharp sword (His word) with which He may strike down the nations, and He will rule them with a rod of iron, and He will tread the winepress of the fierce wrath of God, the Almighty [in the judgment of the rebellious world]* Revelation 19:15 (AMP). In Greek, *logos* means word in the context of theologians. The sword of the spirit is referring to the Bible, called the Word of God by the body of Christ. The logos is what God said. It is past tense, but the Word does not have any limitation. It was created outside of time. *"Jesus Christ is the same yesterday, today, and forever"* Hebrews 13:8 (NKJV). The revelation in this verse is from the words "is the same." He does not change; therefore, Jesus is the Word in which He can be in the past, present, and future. He permanently and forever resides outside of this natural realm. That means the Bible is not just another book with ink dressing up a page; it is spiritual, supernatural, alive, and powerful.

The second is that God's voice is usually an impression that is discerned in the spirit. The voice of God can come to us while praying, worshiping, meditating, or while dreaming. These are the practical things you can do to increase hearing His voice clearly. The voice of God is present and can tell you about the future and past. Both the logos and the voice of God are spirit, and they can release compassion, conviction, activation, impartation, and deposit something into your spirit. God's Words are creative, full of life, and powerful. His words made His imagination a tangible reality. And God said, "*Let there be light: and there was light. And God saw the light, that it was good: and God divided the light from the darkness*" Genesis 1:3–4 (AMP). "*In the beginning [before all-time] was the Word (Christ), and the Word was with God, and the Word was God Himself*" John 1:1 (AMP). The Word is a person, and He is settled in the heavens. The Word can walk, talk, discern, hear, feel, see, and comfort. God is not separate from His Word, just as we cannot separate our soul from our body. The Word of God is a sword, which means it is a weapon that the enemy does not want us to be in union with. Therefore, believers become sleepy, or their mind becomes filled with distractions as they begin to read the Word. The enemy knows the power that is in the Word of God and His voice through revelation that makes you a formidable force

> *The Word of God is living and active and full of power [making it operative, energizing, and effective]. It is sharper than any two-edged sword, penetrating as far as the division of the soul and spirit [the completeness of a person], and of both joints and marrow [the deepest part of our nature], exposing and judging the very thoughts and intentions of the heart.* Hebrews 4:12 (AMP)

Do you remember Luke Skywalker from the *Star Wars* movie in the '80s? The weapon Luke Skywalker used against his nemesis Darth Vader was called a lightsaber. This was a sword of light that cut his enemies in half. The Word of God is not literally a sword that is held in the hand; in the book of Revelation, Christ has a sword in His mouth. Revelation 19:15 (NLT) states it here: From his mouth came a sharp sword to strike down the nations. It says from His mouth comes a sharp sword, which is His Word to confront nations and to rule spiritually. The Word is spirit. It is the breath of God. *"Let your Kingdom come, and your will be done on earth as it is in heaven."* When you declare Matthew 6:33, His kingdom is being established. God's power is word activated; it must be spoken into the atmosphere. Once you say the Word, it creates or manifests the Word. It is like self-rising flour, which does not need any help to increase itself. When we speak God's Word, you are reminding Him of what He said. And He likes that. *"Remind Me [of your merits with a thorough report], let us plead and argue our case together, state your position, that you may be proved right"* Isaiah 43:26 (AMP). God wants us to put Him in remembrance of what He said. *"God is not a man, that he shall lie, or a son of man, that He should change His mind"* Numbers 23:19 (NLT). He is in covenant to His own Word more than to His name. When you speak His Word back to him, that is saying you are engaging with His Word, He has your undivided attention, and He has priority in your life. *"My people are destroyed for lack of knowledge"* Hosea 4:6. If you are being destroyed in an area such as finances, health, marriage, ministry, and so forth, there is knowledge you are missing. By establishing the Word in your life in that area, you can change your finances and other areas to success. *And these signs will accompany those who believe in My name, they will cast out demons, they shall speak new tongues. They will pick up serpents, and if they drink anything deadly, it will not hurt them; they will lay hands on the sick, and they will get well* Mark 16:17–18 (NIV).

When we believe His words and declare them as truth, He himself will accompany us with signs to affirm our relationship with Him. The Word of God is His "Constitution." His Word supernaturally carries so much weight in the spirit that He names it a sword, which is an offensive and defensive weapon. That is why in Revelation it says, "a sword in His mouth." You can cut people with words; there is life and death in the tongue. *Behold, I give you authority to tread upon serpents and scorpions, and overall, the power of the enemy; and nothing shall by any means hurt you* Luke 10:19 (NKJV). God is telling us we possess authority and the ability to exercise and execute authority over all of Satan's power. His

Word does not return to Him void; it always comes back to Him with profits of equity. *"When you decree a thing, it shall be established, and light will shine on your path";* hence, the biblical meaning for light. This is scripture from Job 22:28 (NKJV)

Light

Beyond the physical element, light in the Bible stands for spiritual illumination and truth. It encompasses all that is pure, good, and holy, as opposed to the darkness of evil. God's Word is *"a lamp for my feet and a light for my path"* (Ps. 119:105). It guides us in following His commands throughout our lives. The Bible says *"And no wonder, for Satan himself masquerades as an angel of light"* 2 Corinthians 11:14 (NIV). You could trust him because you mistakenly think he is an angel sent by God. Therefore, the Bible says that when anyone who comes to you, it's important to test the spirit.

Truth

Truth is opposed to what is feigned, fictitious, and false. When we follow and obey the Word of God, it is impossible for us to lose. The Word of God is timeless, boundless, limitless, and everlasting; it was made to work and manifest in time and in the spirit. When you read the Word, the Word reads you. You may begin to sob, feel remorse for what you have done in the past, feel a sense of joy and closeness to the Lord, or feel His presence. The Word makes you question yourself. It makes you examine your own heart. *"For the Word of God is alive and active. Sharper than any double-edged sword, it penetrates even to dividing soul and spirit, joints and marrow; it judges the thoughts and attitudes of the heart"* Hebrews 4:12 (NIV).

6. The Shield of Faith

Faith is not for the future. Everything about God is now. In the book of Genesis 1:3 (NKJV), scripture says, *"Then God said, let there be light, and there was light."* What God spoke happened simultaneously without delay. It happened right then and there. In the mind of God, He wanted the opposite of what He saw in front of Him. Our faith must follow suit. It does not exist if it's not spoken in this realm. God does not need faith because He is naturally supernatural. Faith was created for the natural realm. Faith is a portal for the supernatural to invade. *"Now Faith is the substance of things hoped for, the evidence of things not seen"* Hebrews 11:1 (KJV). Faith is not about the past nor is it about the future. Faith is present in the now, an immediate manifestation. Faith requires a course of action. Faith's attraction to you is by movement. Faith without works is dead. Faith requires you to do something. For example, when unemployed, you tell everyone you want a job, but you stay home and do not even send out resumes by email. How can you find a job or who will recommend you for employment? Going to sleep late and waking up at 2 p.m. daily cuts the amount of productive time that is available for you to find a job.

With no action to acquire or obtain a job, you will always be unemployed months or even years later, until there is action to your words that you want a job. As a woman with an exceptional fragrance captivates a man's full attention, in the same way, faith allures God to manifest Himself on your behalf. Our faith arouses the Creator of heaven and earth. *"But without faith, it is impossible to please him; for he that cometh to God must believe that he is, and that he is a rewarder of them that diligently seek him"* Hebrews 11: 6 (KJV). Outside of the realm of faith, we are not pleasing to God, and He is not content or satisfied. When we are in fear, unbelief, doubt, reason, and worry, we are outside the realm of faith. These enemies of faith can paralyze, neutralize, and naturalize the things of God. *"But he who is uncertain [about eating a particular thing] is condemned if he eats because he is not acting from faith. Whatever is not from faith is sin [whatever is done with doubt is sinful]."* Romans 14:23 (AMP)

As the above verse says, whatever is not from faith is a sin; making decisions from our emotions, feelings, or fear is a sin. Our emotions and feelings are not stable; they are up and down, based on the situation or circumstances in our lives. Faith is not unstable; it is absolute. Fear is a spirit that is False Evidence Appearing Real, and fear is the perversion of faith. When we act out of faith, we take an action and move; when we act out of fear, action is hindered and paralyzed. Fear, stress, and anxiety are demonic weapons used against humankind and meant to release destruction 1 Timothy 6:12. *"Fight the good fight of faith."* This implies that there is a war, battle, or an opponent. To win this fight, you must be defensive and offensive minded. The armor of God is replicated of the Roman soldiers' uniform and their weapons. The shield was one of the weapons they carried. It was wood and drenching it with water kept it wet, protecting it by making it supple from the enemy's arrows that had fire and poison on its tip. That is the defensive method the Romans used for wetting their shield was to dilute the poison and quench the fire. Also, if a soldier was in close combat, they used their shield as an offensive weapon to push back or hit the enemy in close range. Therefore, the shield of faith is so important for us to have as part of our warfare garment, ready for war. The enemy is constantly surveilling, monitoring, and studying you to see what is in your life that resembles him. Once he can identify a reflection of himself in you; he will use it against you. His goal is to devour you. Malachi 3:11 (KJV) gives us hope about this type of situation: *"And I will rebuke the devourer for your sake, and he shall not destroy the fruits of your ground."*

Jesus made a statement; none of Satan is found in me. In John 14:30 (NKJV), he tells the disciples, *"I will no longer talk much with you, for the ruler of this world is coming, and he has nothing in me."* When seeing where you are weak, the devil comes to steal, kill, and destroy your life, whether you are saved or not. *"Put on the full armor of God [for His precepts are like the splendid armor of a heavily-armed soldier], so that you may be able to [successfully] stand up against all the schemes and the strategies and the deceits of the devil"* Ephesians 6:11(AMP).

Within that verse, God wants us to put on the full armor of God. It qualifies us to stand, stand firm, and stand against the schemes, strategies, wiles, tricks, and tactics of the devil. That is why we need the shield of faith for supernatural defense. It is an offensive weapon against demonic and diabolical attacks from death, violence, anger, aggression, witchcraft, perversion, Jezebel and Delilah spirits, occult, religion, and many more. What is the shield of faith? How do you get the shield of faith? When are we supposed to use it? Where do we get the shield of faith from? These are questions we have wondered; the answers are in the scriptures. The combat we are in is supernatural, not natural. The natural eyes cannot see the things of the spirit. *"But the natural man does not receive the things of the spirit of God, for they are foolish to him; nor can he know them, because they are spiritually discerned"* 1 Corinthians 2:14 (NKJV).

Faith is the beginning of the supernatural. Therefore, faith is the prerequisite or introduction to obtaining spiritual things in this natural realm. The shield of faith is part of the armor of God, a spiritual garment that requires discernment. It also requires you to believe you have a weapon and protection. The shield of faith permits you to have a defense and yet still have an offense mentality. The things of God are Word activated. By faith, we declare with our mouth, "I hold the shield of faith." Whenever you know you are going into a dangerous situation, atmosphere, neighborhood, or house in prayer where there may be warfare, grab your shield for battle. Before you leave your house, take the shield into your hands, and declare that you are surrounded by the shield of faith in your home, on your property, in your vehicle, and so forth, and that no demonic weapon formed against you shall prosper. *"So then faith comes by hearing; and hearing by the Word of God"* Romans 10:17 (KJV). Hearing requires action. Once you hear a revelation from God, do it. The Word of God releases faith because the Word is spirit. The spirit of faith is fed by hearing the Word. The nourishment for faith is the Word of God. Your faith cannot grow if you only have an appetizer of the Word. You must immerse yourself in the Word. The intimacy with the Word of God will determine your level of faith in the realm of the supernatural. Also, intimacy with the spirit of God will make you an atomic bomb in the spirit realm. Faith is not a myth nor a legend. Jesus is the Author and Finisher of our faith Hebrews 12:2. Our faith comes from Jesus; He is the Word that became flesh. No casting out demons was manifested until Jesus brought the kingdom of God. The key to the kingdom of God is having faith. Having the revelation of faith will move mountains. Faith can be felt, seen, heard, and experienced like Jesus did.

7. The Spirit of God

For your armor to be effective, you need one more part of the armor that brings completion. This is the Spirit of God. The Spirit of God is the activator of every part of the armor of God. The armor of God works through the ministry of the Spirit of God who works together with believers to accomplish their supernatural mission. And it is the Spirit of God that gives us the revelation of the armor of God. *"For you created my inmost being you knit me together in my mother's womb"* Psalm 139:13 (NIV). God did not physically do it with His hands but by His Spirit. In Genesis 1:2 (KJV), scripture says *"And the earth was without form, and void, and the darkness was upon the face of the deep. And the spirit of God moved upon the face of the waters."* Before God came on the scene, there was formlessness, darkness, and emptiness. Then He spoke. The Spirit of God hovered to cultivate, induce, impregnate, and prepare the atmosphere, frequencies, and airwaves upon the face of the earth. The Spirit of God has many names, and the most common one is the Holy Spirit, but here are some of the others:

- The breath of God scriptures of the Holy Spirit for each
- Breath of the Almighty

- Counselor and Comforter
- Eternal Spirit
- Power of the Highest
- The Spirit of might
- The Spirit of adoption
- Spirit of Christ
- Spirit of Glory
- Spirit of Grace
- Spirit of Truth
- The Spirit of revelation

God Himself wants us to know how valuable the Spirit of God is to the Godhead. Do you remember Genesis 2:7 (KJV): *"And the Lord God formed man of the dust of the ground and breathed into his nostrils the breath of life, and man became a living soul"*? Most of us have attended a funeral service and have seen the body of a family member, loved one, or friend lifeless in a casket. Without the spirit of God in man, there is no life; the essence of our being is the spirit of God in us. God breathed life into Adam's nostrils. As God is in heaven, so was Adam upon the earth. Man became a living being to rule and reign in the Garden of Eden. In God's mind, the armor of God is ineffective without the Spirit of God. That is why it is the final piece in the armor of God. It is the Spirit who connects, activates, and seals the armor so there is no breach in combat. I have learned personally that once your armor is on, begin to pray in the Spirit. What is needed to empower each part of the armor will then be enhanced to its highest capacity and sensitivity. Here is a testimony of a disciple of mine. Monday nights at our church is prayer, and as we were praying and worshiping in the spirit (in tongues), one of our pastors said from the altar, "Put on the full armor of God." We began warfare by praying in tongues. During that time, my disciple had an open vision (spiritual) of the armor of God upon him. He described it as shiny and gleaming, looking very masculine and aggressive. He saw a man with a gun, and he ran; as he was running, he fell. The man opened fire with a gun at point-blank range and pumped six to seven shots into his chest. The amazing thing is he was experiencing the bullets bouncing off the breastplate. He was not harmed in any way in the vision (spiritual).

That incident gave him the revelation of how valuable the armor of God is to us as sons and daughters of God. So, putting on the armor of God before leaving the house every morning is paramount. Anywhere you go, you can activate the armor of God on you. Do not be religious about it, but always be in the spirit; there are no limits to the things in the spirit. The armor of God is activated by the Spirit of God. The spirit of peace relates to the shoes, the spirit of truth with the belt, the spirit of righteousness with the breastplate, the spirit of salvation with the helmet, the sword of the spirit with the sword, and the spirit of faith with the shield. The armor itself is spiritual and needs faith to place it into action, but what brings it to life is the Holy Spirit. Jesus went to the cross and died for the sins of humanity so the spirit of Jesus would be everywhere. He wanted every human being to carry God inside. Christians know He (Jesus) is inside of us, but the unbelievers don't know He is inside of them. God is not a man, but a spirit; we are made in the image and likeness of God. Therefore, if we pray in the spirit, we will be just like God. In Psalm 82:6 (NKJV) scripture *"I said, you are gods; you are all sons of the Most High,"* all of you." The greatest desire of God in heaven is for His sons and daughters on earth to be like Him. *"Therefore, become imitators of God (copy Him and follow His example), as well-beloved children (imitate their Father)"* Ephesian 5:1 (AMP).

God wants us to be heaven on earth in the same way Jesus was for us to follow. "Let your kingdom come on earth as it is in heaven and give us our daily bread" is the verse that proves this. The Holy Spirit makes all things very noticeable once He is involved. He heightens that area, for example, compassion, conviction, discernment, love, forgiveness, faith, and so forth. Once I had knowledge of the Holy Spirit, I began to forgive people. I had more compassion for people who were not saved and those who were experiencing life hardships and the loss of a loved one. The Spirit of God will expose an area where you are not imitating Him. He will let you know you are not like the Father in this area and repentance is needed to reestablish you in right standing with God. The executive administrator of the Godhead or Trinity is the Holy Spirit. Nothing that manifests from the spirit is without the Holy Spirit. *"Then he answered and spoke unto me, saying, this is the word of the Lord unto Zerubbabel, saying, not by might, nor by power, but by my spirit, said the Lord of the hosts"* Zechariah 4:6 (KJV).

I encourage you to put on the armor of God and pray in the spirit (pray in tongues). Everything from God comes from His Spirit who serves us and is against the works and wiles of darkness. This is the moment you must ask yourself, are you giving God service with the talents and gifts He gave you? Are you serving in the house of God? We are called not to neglect the assembly of the brethren. What servility have you given to your community, society, or your family? God takes an account of all the works you are doing on earth, and they will be tested by fire.

Prayer of Repentance

Father God, forgive me for not being a servant and not serving in all the capacities I could have served in life. I repent for not having Your heart and the heart of servitude. I ask for the blood of Jesus to wash and cleanse me. I renounce the spirit of laziness, familiarity, pride, independence, selfishness, self-righteousness, and self-centeredness. Father God, give me the grace in servanthood to love. Give me the strength to serve, and humbleness and peace to imitate Jesus Christ. I thank you, Holy Spirit, for revealing my destiny to become a blessing through servanthood and for showing me the purpose of my life is to serve. In Jesus's mighty name. Amen.

Activation of Servanthood

I declare over the reader of this book that the spirit of grace of servanthood be release over you. May the spirit of servanthood be activated in your spiritual walk with the Lord God. I empower you to serve God, your parents, pastors, and children. Your destiny, purpose, and calling be revealed as you serve the Lord God. I prophesy that your chosen season comes as you serve and be a blessing to the body of Christ. Amen

Thank you for reading my book and may it edify your spirit man.

Alison Marcellus is an ordained minister, author, and preacher that preach the word of God with power through the holy spirit. I am currently a student at the University of the Supernatural Ministry in Miami Florida.

CPSIA information can be obtained
at www.ICGtesting.com
Printed in the USA
BVHW052042020323
659568BV00002B/2